Famous Tales From Turkey

With Activities for the Primary Classroom

Barry Nicholson

Starhands Publishing

Famous Tales From Turkey

Copyright © 2015 Barry Nicholson. All rights reserved.

First paperback edition printed 2015.

A catalogue record for this book is available from the British Library.

ISBN: 9780993243813

ISBN: 0993243819

Published by Starhands Publishing.

www.starhandspublishing.co.uk

Printed in the United States

Famous Tales From Turkey: Locations

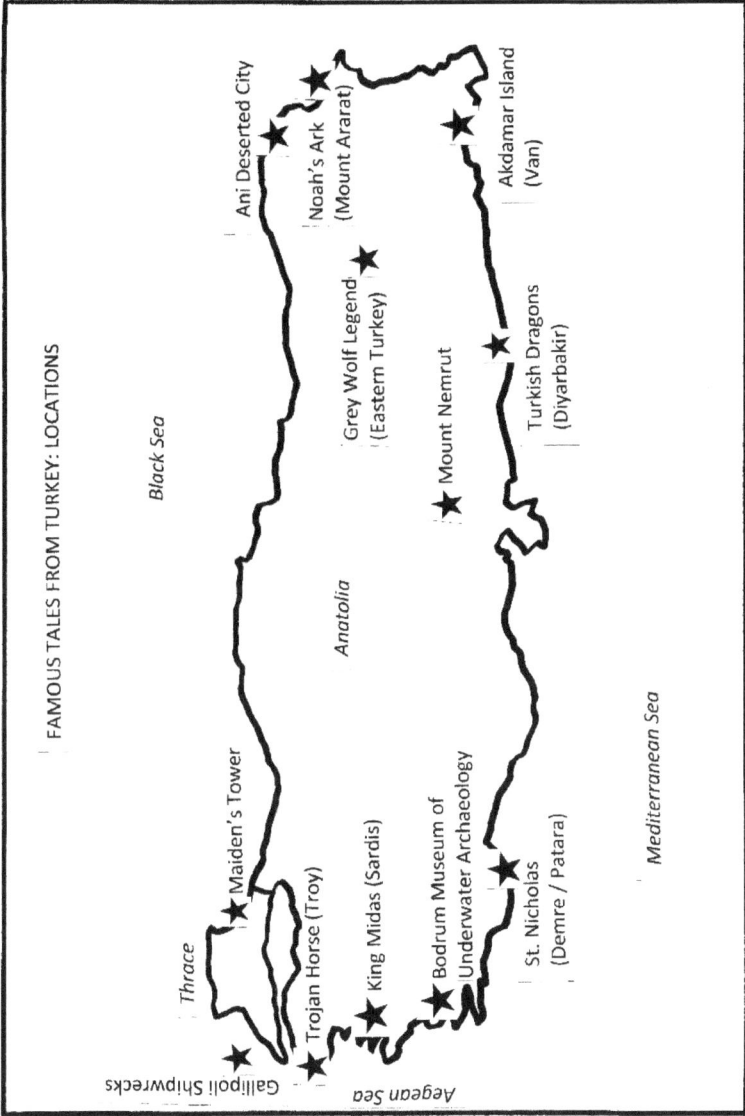

Black Sea

Anatolia

Thrace

Aegean Sea

Mediterranean Sea

Ani Deserted City

Noah's Ark (Mount Ararat)

Akdamar Island (Van)

Grey Wolf Legend (Eastern Turkey)

Mount Nemrut

Turkish Dragons (Diyarbakir)

Maiden's Tower

Trojan Horse (Troy)

King Midas (Sardis)

Bodrum Museum of Underwater Archaeology

St. Nicholas (Demre / Patara)

Gallipoli Shipwrecks

BARRY NICHOLSON

CONTENTS

BARRY NICHOLSON

LIST OF ACTIVITIES

BARRY NICHOLSON

INTRODUCTION

Most of us have heard of the Wooden Horse of Troy, Saint Nicholas, or King Midas and his golden touch. But did you know that they all come from what is modern day Turkey?

Turkey has such a rich history and tradition, and tales such as these lie at the heart of this magical culture. Everywhere you turn there is history and legend, built upon foundations of the past. A rich and diverse heritage cannot be missed, and I urge you to visit Turkey if you have not done so already. You will find not only splendid Ottoman architecture, but also remnants of Greek and Roman occupation, of Christians, Iranians and Armenians.

This book has been written with children in mind. Children love tales of legend and mystery, especially when connected with historical characters or animals. Within these pages you will find a wealth of interesting and intriguing characters, both human and animal. Add to that the remains of ancient cities and culture and you have a recipe for success.

I like the idea of this book because it links legends and tales from Turkey to actual practical activities for the classroom. I think that this is the primary strength of the book: it turns the academic into the practical, the intangible asset of a cultural story or tale into a real-life and concrete end result. The idea of turning theory into practice is especially important for teaching children, who often need a concrete visualisation of a tale or legend so that it sticks in their mind and they learn from it.

That's why there are suggested activities at the end of each chapter. Some of the activities are fun, some are games, some involve drawing or colouring, maybe a speaking activity such as role-play, or a song. The aim is to try to give the tales a 3D feel, to bring them to life, and create engagement with the children. Each activity is different, and their purpose is to suggest to the teacher or parent a method of extending the tale into the real world. One of the activities challenges the reader and his friends to a treasure hunt, collecting objects listed from their home or school. One is a quiz about the grey wolf, to be played on one's own or with friends. Another challenges the children to make their own dragon from paper, or to make their very own Trojan Horse from card.

There are twelve chapters in this book and each focusses on a tale or set of tales, often with some kind of moral. The twelve chapters are:

- *The Wooden Horse of Troy*: this story signifies that trickery can be used in order to win a cause or battle, and echoes the saying 'beware of Greeks bearing gifts';
- *King Midas and his Golden Touch*: the moral of this story is that greed can cause you to lose everything you hold close to your heart;
- *Saint Nicholas and the Three Pickled Boys*: Saint Nicholas is known for his generosity to those in need, and his love for children;
- *The Grey Wolf Legend*: the legend of the grey wolf Ashina (Asena) is an old Turkic myth that tells how the Turkic people were created;
- *Turkish Sky Dragons*: they have a major symbolic role as they bring rain, prosperity and power;

- *Maiden's Castle, Istanbul*: this story shows how love in extreme can actually have a negative effect;
- *Akdamar Island, Van*: just like Romeo and Juliet, Akdamar Island has a lover's tale of its own;
- *The Deserted Ghost City of Ani*: some cities are alive, others fade away into history and lie in ruins for the adventurous to explore;
- *Mount Nemrut's Statues of the Past*: as royal tombs go, the constructions at Mount Nemrut are spectacular not only for their size but also for their stunning location;
- *Noah's Ark, Mount Ararat*: when Noah built an ark to escape the floods, it settled on Mount Ararat in eastern Turkey;
- *Sunken History: Gallipoli Shipwrecks*: anyone interested in First World War history or diving in the sea will have a fine time around the Gallipoli Peninsula;
- *Bodrum Museum of Underwater Archaeology*: St. Peter's Castle is home to one of the most important museums in the world.

I have personally been to a lot of the sites in this book, especially those in western Turkey that are far more accessible. Some information came from these site visits, but much of the material has come from the internet, and a final section gives credit to the various websites and some brief information on them. Go to these websites if you'd like any more details in addition to what I present here.

And, of course, don't forget to create materials and ideas of your own!

Barry Nicholson
Istanbul 2015

1.
THE WOODEN HORSE OF TROY

BARRY NICHOLSON

1. THE WOODEN HORSE OF TROY

The story of the Wooden Horse of Troy signifies trickery in order to win a cause or battle, and echoes the saying 'beware of Greeks bearing gifts'.

But did the ancient city of Troy and the wooden horse actually exist, or is it all just a myth? Until the 1800s it was thought to be just that – a myth – until the German archaeologist Heinrich Schliemann came across what is now thought to be the remains of the ancient city of Troy. It is located near the modern-day city of Canakkale in western Turkey (Thrace).

Long ago, there were a number of attempts to establish the city, at least seven, but fires, invasions and earthquakes led to successive destruction of the city. It was the seventh attempt, Troy VII, that the Greeks invaded during the Trojan War with the help of their wooden horse.

The Greeks and Trojans had fought for a long time without any success on either side. The Greek warriors had won many important battles but could not breach the sturdy walls around Troy, and neither could the Trojans drive the Greeks away. It was the Greek King Odysseus of Ithaca who had the idea to build a wooden horse. The horse was hollow and built on wheels, big enough for an army of thirty Greek soldiers to hide inside. It was built by Epeius, a master carpenter. The plan was for the Greek army to pretend to sail away in defeat, but to leave the horse (still full of soldiers) near the city of Troy.

One man, Sinon, was left behind. When the Trojans arrived to see the huge horse, Sinon pretended to be angry with the Greeks, saying that they had deserted him. He persuaded the Trojans that the horse would bring good luck, and they should offer it to the God Athena. So as to not upset the God, they dragged the horse into the city of Troy. The horse was so big that they had to tear down part of the city walls to get it in. The horse was left at the Temple of Athena as an offering to please the God.

But their celebration of victory was misguided. Whilst the Trojans slept, the army of Greek soldiers rushed out from inside and killed every Trojan in sight. Their friends who had 'sailed away' in their ships came back to reinforce them and, after a big battle, the Greeks finally won.

No trace of the original horse exists, though it is possible to see reconstructions in the area today. One, at the site of Troy itself, stands around twenty metres high and is made of wooden planks. Visitors can climb a steep staircase and go inside the horse. A second reconstruction is on the seafront promenade in Canakkale. Though you can't climb up inside it, its straw-like construction is said by many to be more of a likeness to the original.

Visitors to the Thrace area of western Turkey can still see the remains of the city of Troy, though some imagination is required as the remains are incomplete and mangled. Most impressive are the remains of the walls of Troy VII; though these are only around forty metres long and five metres high, they provide a good image of the fortifications the wooden horse had to scale.

To get to Troy, the modern city of Canakkale is your starting point. You need to locate the dolmus (minibus) station below the bridge that crosses the river, then take one of the hourly minibuses to Troy (Truva). It only takes about thirty minutes. There are few facilities at the site, so take a packed lunch, and as the site is very exposed try not to visit if it is windy or the weather is inclement. There is a small entry fee. As you enter the site a large wooden horse greets you, and after climbing up into it you can tour the city of Troy in an anti-clockwise direction. There is a small gift shop for souvenirs and guidebooks.

Idea for the Classroom: Trojan Horse Play

It is possible to write and perform a play about the Trojan Horse, and there are certainly enough characters (soldiers, Greeks, Trojans, Gods) for everyone to have a part. The only difficulty might be finding enough speaking parts: the Greeks can have lines such as "let's build a wooden horse and trick the Trojans" or the Trojans might say "what's that? A wooden horse?". Gods can be happy ("You did well to build your wooden horse"), authoritative ("Go build your wooden horse") or angry ("If you don't take the horse into the city, I will be angry").

There is also a lot of scope for costumes, and I suspect a lot of competition to be selected and dressed up as a God. Use old curtains as robes, and make swords and daggers from cardboard. If the drama is good enough, get the children to perform in front of their schoolmates or parents. Here is a sample play script:

The Trojan Horse

Characters

Greek Soldier 1
Greek Soldier 2
Trojan Soldier 1
Trojan Soldier 2
God 1

God 2
Wooden Horse
Trojan villagers

Situation

Ancient Thrace, rolling green hills and sparse trees, birds sing in the background. There is a mighty stone fortification.

Script

Greeks stand on the left, Trojans stand on the right.

Greek Soldier 1: I hate the Trojans!
Trojan Soldier 1: I hate the Greeks!
All Greek Soldiers: We hate the Trojans!
All Trojan Soldiers: We hate the Greeks!

The soldiers fight.

Greek Soldier 2: Let's pretend to go home in our ships.
Greek Soldier 1: Good idea.
Greek Soldier 2: We can make a wooden horse. It will confuse them.
Greek Soldier 1: We can trick them. We can win.

The Greeks leave a wooden horse, then pretend to sail away in their ships.

Wooden Horse: Hello, I'm a wooden horse. I am not empty. I am full of Greek soldiers. We will trick the Trojans.
Trojan Soldier 1: What's this?
Trojan Soldier 2: A wooden horse.
God 1: Take the horse into your city. If you don't, we will be angry.
God 2: If you don't, we will be very angry!
Trojan Soldier 1: Let's take the horse into the city.

Trojan Soldier 2: Yes, then the Gods will not be angry.

Later, in the city...

Wooden Horse: All the soldiers inside me are very quiet.
Suddenly...
All Greek Soldiers: Charge! Kill the Trojans!
Greek Soldier 1: Look! Our friends from the ship are here!
All Greek Soldiers: Charge! Kill the Trojans!

They fight. All the Trojans are killed.

All Greek Soldiers: We won! Hooray!
God 1: It was an interesting fight.
God 2: Yes, better than watching television!

All actors take a bow.

Idea for the classroom: Trojan Horse Handicraft

Another use in the classroom is to make a wooden horse out of cardboard, paper, egg boxes and the like. Each child can make their own horse if you have enough materials, or you could make it group work, or make one big horse as a class. Below I provide an example template for you to copy, in which you can insert the six body parts into slits cut into a toilet tube.

Trojan Horse Template

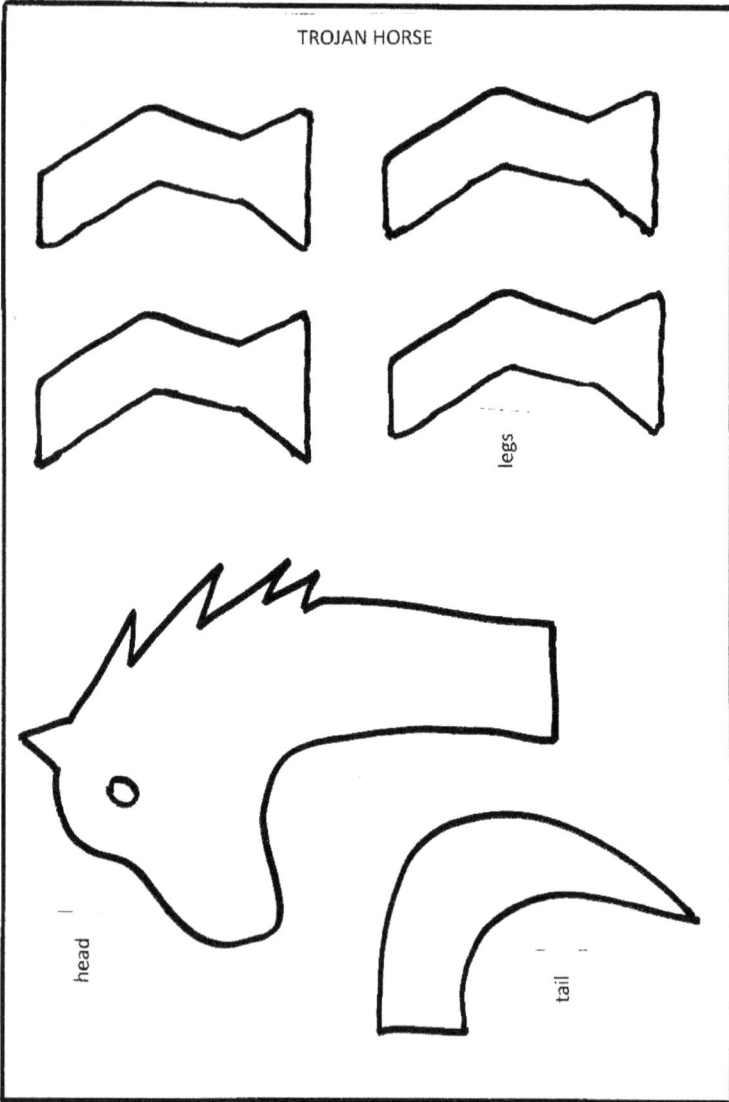

TROJAN HORSE

legs

head

tail

Idea for the Classroom: Animals ABC Game

This is a very simplistic thinking and writing activity which can be used to introduce the topic of animals in general, or as a gap filler.

Write or type the letters of the alphabet down the left side of a piece of paper. In groups, the challenge is to find an animal that starts with each of the letters. Who can finish first? Some are very easy, for example 'c - cat' or 'm - monkey', but others require thought, for example 'u - ugly frog'. Below are the results from one of my classes as an example of the finished product.

Ant
Baboon
Cat
Dog
Elephant
Flappy bird
Goat
Hippo
Ice bear
Jellyfish
Kangaroo
Lion
Monkey
Newt
Octopus
Porcupine
Queen bee
Rabbit
Snake
Tiger
Ugly frog
Very big elephant
Whale
X-ray vision eagle
Yellow canary
Zebra

2.
KING MIDAS
AND HIS
GOLDEN TOUCH

BARRY NICHOLSON

2. KING MIDAS
AND HIS GOLDEN TOUCH

The moral of this story is that greed can cause you to lose everything you hold close to your heart.

A long time ago there was a wealthy king called Midas. He loved money and gold, and would spend hours in his golden room counting out his gold coins. The king grew so fond of his treasure that he loved it more than anything else in the world. And still he wanted more.

One day an old traveller, Silenus, got drunk and passed out in the king's rose garden at the palace. He was brought to the king. Midas recognised him as a follower of the god Dionysus (the God of wine, revelry and celebration) and so treated him to a ten-day feast.

After this banquet, Midas brought Silenus safely back to the god Dionysus who was very grateful for his return. Dionysus offered to grant King Midas a single wish in return for his kindness, so Midas wished that whatever he touched should turn into gold. Dionysus granted the wish, and the next day when the king woke, all he touched would turn to gold.

The next day came, and he was eager to try out his new power. Indeed, when he touched his bed it turned to gold; when he touched his chair it turned to gold; and when he touched his table it turned to gold too. What magical powers! The king was delighted!

However, when he sat down to breakfast he realised his mistake. When he picked up bread to eat, it turned a hard, yellow and shiny gold! And when he tried to drink water, it too turned to gold! Suddenly his beloved daughter entered the room, but when he hugged her, she too turned into a gold statue. He started to sense fear. If everything he touched turned to gold, how could he eat or drink? How could he love his daughter?

In despair, he prayed again to the god Dionysus. Thankfully, Dionysus heard him and told him to bathe in the waters of the River Pactolus and this would remove the wish-turned-curse. As Midas bathed in the Pactolus, he was astonished to see golden water flowing from his hands: as he bathed, the power of the golden touch flowed out of him and into the water. The river became speckled with gold! When he sprinkled water from the river onto the golden objects, they returned to normal. Even his daughter returned to normal, who he hugged in happiness.

He decided that from that day on, he would share his wealth and not be selfish. King Midas became a better person, and when he died all his people mourned for their beloved king.

The River Pactolus is located in the Izmir region in modern-day Turkey. It is reputed to still have a golden sparkle to this day.

Some say the tale took part at Sardis (Sart) in western Turkey near the modern cities of Izmir and Manisa. I didn't see much of a golden sparkle when I visited, but it is an interesting place nonetheless. Sardis is also reputed to be where the first gold coins were minted, which is perhaps why the Midas tale has historically been connected with Sardis.

King Midas has become legendary, but his tale survives only in a figure of speech – one speaks of "the Midas touch", suggesting that true wealth is intangible and proverbial.

To visit Sardis it is best to have private transport. Take the E-96 road east of Izmir towards Salihli (the road then goes on to Usak). Half way between Ahmetli and Salihli you will see Sardis signed on your right. It is also possible to travel by express bus from Izmir to Salihli, then back-track for the thirty minute journey by minibus.

Sardis itself is divided into two sites: one partly reconstructed Roman site near the main road, and a second more evocative site about a kilometre away from the main road with a ruined (but very impressive) Temple of Apollo. One modest entrance fee covers both sites.

There is a river in the valley below but unfortunately there are no traces of gold and the waters appear rather murky. Is this where King Midas bathed? I can't see it, personally. No sign of a rose garden either. A better option for the adventurous is to trek into the jagged mountains above the temple. There are several signed paths that eventually lead the visitor up to a small hermitage and viewpoint.

Idea for the Classroom: Scavenger Hunt

Taking the idea of kings, queens and royalty further, a good option for an extension activity is to stage a scavenger hunt.

For this you need a number of royalty-related items, and an area to stage the event such as a garden or playground. Items might be a plastic sword, crown, or diamond necklace for example. About twenty objects should keep the children occupied, and make sure you hide the items so that they can be found only with some determined searching.

Divide your children into two teams, and instruct them to find the items within a given time limit. You can present the items as a list, like the one below; some extra objects are added for fun. The team that collects the most is the winner, and are awarded winning badges.

Scavenger Hunt

You have thirty minutes.
How many of these things can you find?

1. plastic sword
2. golden crown
3. diamond necklace
4. diamond ring
5. photo of a castle
6. soft toy horse
7. soldier toy figure
8. golden apple
9. loaf of bread
10. bunch of grapes
11. king's robe
12. book of fairy tales
13. feather
14. pot of gold
15. pack of cards
16. gold coin
17. rose made of paper
18. photo of a princess
19. glass of river water
20. one more thing related to royalty

Idea for the Classroom: Treasure Chest Collage

By now your learners will be familiar with the story of King Midas and may be wondering what it is like to have such a lot of gold and treasure. Now's their chance! A picture is worth a thousand words, and children often learn better with visual imagery. Creating a treasure chest collage allows children to use their imagination and make a striking work of visual imagery for any classroom wall.

Start with a large piece of coloured paper and draw on it the basic box shape of a treasure chest. An alternative is to find an old cardboard box that you can paint or decorate to look like a chest. The idea is to make some treasure to fill the chest: photocopies of toy money that the children can colour, shiny diamonds and jewels, gold coins and necklaces. As the objects are added to the chest, a mighty box of treasure is created.

Glossy magazines are a good source of pictures of jewellery, or you could use the money templates below to help you.

Idea for the Classroom: Paper Crowns

Would you like to be a king or queen for the day? Yes? Then why not make your own decorative crown? Your crown can be used in a role-play, in a game of Kings & Queens, or as part of a costume to a party. What's more, a paper crown is very easy to make. All you need is some coloured A4 paper, crayons, scissors, and tape or glue. On a sheet of A4 paper, draw a zig-zag line down the middle (example below). Cut down the line to make two halves, then stick or tape the two halves together. Use colours to decorate the crown with diamonds, rubies, and gold. It's that simple! Now who looks like King Midas?

Treasure Chest Money

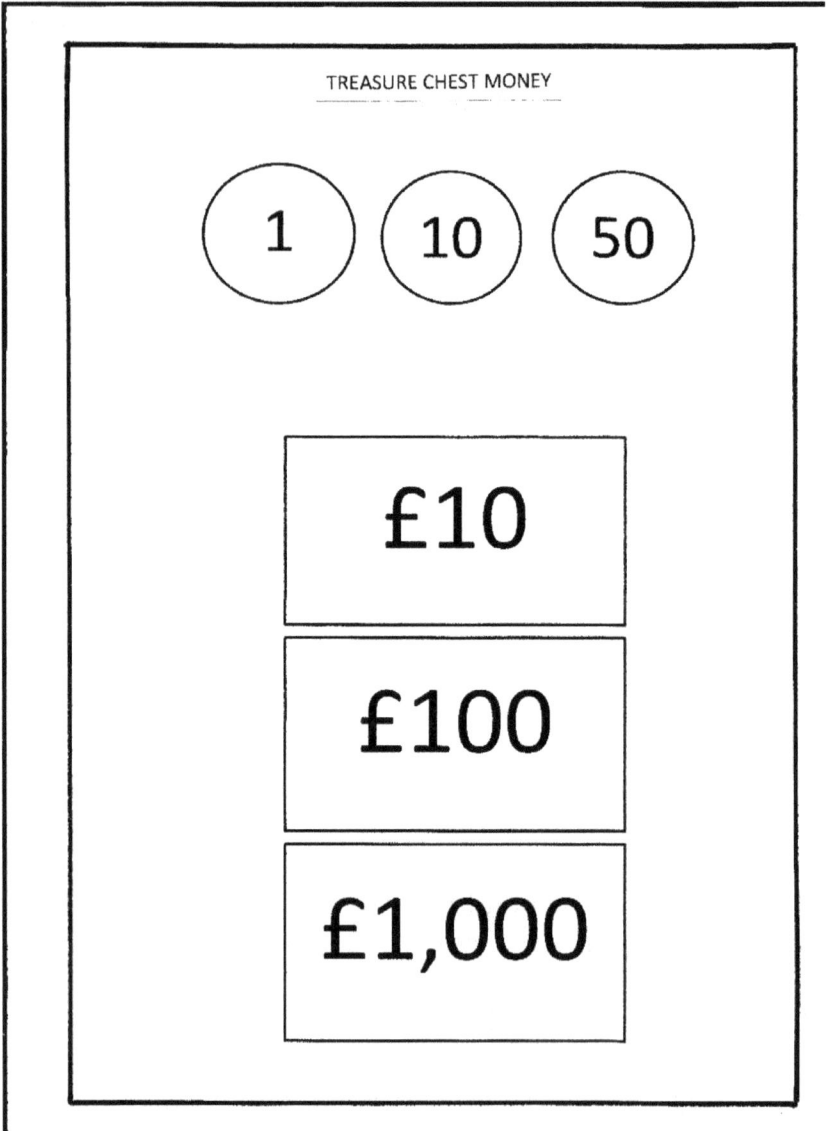

TREASURE CHEST MONEY

(1) (10) (50)

£10

£100

£1,000

Paper Crown Template

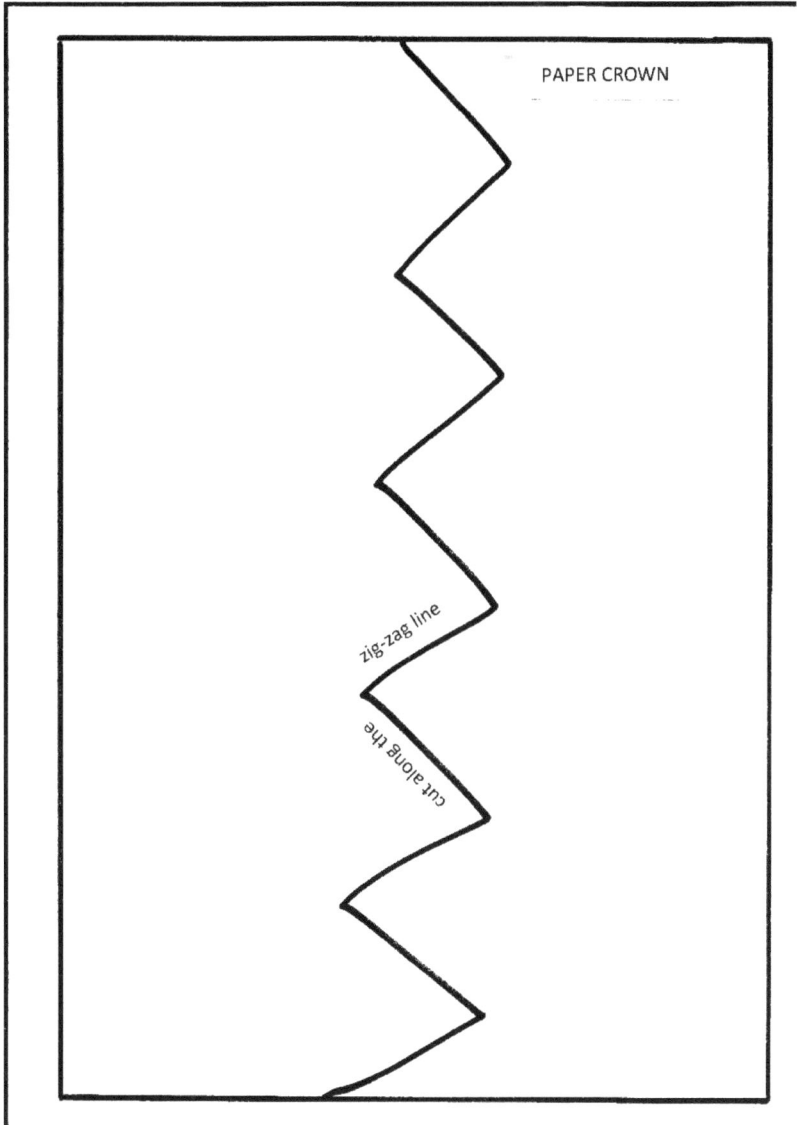

PAPER CROWN

zig-zag line

cut along the

BARRY NICHOLSON

3.
SAINT NICHOLAS
AND THE
THREE PICKLED BOYS

BARRY NICHOLSON

3. ST NICHOLAS
AND THE THREE PICKLED BOYS

Saint Nicholas is known for his generosity for those in need, and his love for children. Nicholas is the patron and protector of children.

He was born in Patara, formerly a port on the Mediterranean Sea, and then part of the Roman Empire. This area is now on the southern coast of Turkey. Nicholas was an only son and he was very religious from an early age. Unfortunately, his parents died from an epidemic outbreak when he was still a boy, but he pledged to use his inheritance to help the needy and sick - especially children.

Many astonishing miracles have been attributed to him, and he is also known as 'Saint Nicholas the Wonder-Worker'. He became the Bishop of Myra (southern Turkey) at a young age and he is often referred to as the 'Boy Bishop'.

A popular example of his extraordinary character is the tale of the three pickled boys. The story goes that during a terrible famine a wicked butcher lured three young children into his house where he killed them. The butcher placed their remains in a barrel to pickle and cure them, planning to sell them off as cured ham and mince pies! Saint Nicholas happened to be visiting the region at the time, and saw through the butcher's crime. By prayer, he was able to resurrect the three boys and bring them back to life.

Another variation of the story is that three theological students, travelling on their way to study in Athens, were robbed and murdered by a wicked innkeeper who hid their remnants in a large pickling tub. Nicholas happened to be at that very inn, and at night he dreamt of the crime. He got up and confronted the innkeeper. As Nicholas prayed to God with all his heart, the three young men were restored to life and returned to their families.

Tales like these explain why Saint Nicholas is the patron and protector of children. Throughout the world he is praised, often under the guise of Santa Claus. After the destruction of World War II, Santa Claus became a symbol of generosity as American troops, dressed as Santa, gave treats to children. He therefore became associated with good things in children's minds.

In Canterbury, England, there is an annual parade though the city's medieval streets in honour of Saint Nicholas. It takes place on St Nicholas Day, December 6th. Adults and children alike dress the part and make their way through cheering crowds. When I visited Canterbury recently, the Cathedral Shop offered a stylish tree decoration of Saint Nicholas, and a leather bookmark depicting the three naked boys in a cooking pot - obviously with an element of humour!

To get to modern day Patara or Demre (formerly Myra), your starting point is the resort city of Antalya. Express buses ply their way south-west from Antalya down the scenic coast. Get off at Demre for the main Nicholas tourist spot, or continue west to Kalkan to view the vast beach at Patara. If your budget suits, the most pleasing way to get to Demre is by boat. You can join a launch at either Antalya or Fethiye or one of the smaller harbours inbetween. These 'Blue Cruise' boats are expensive, and you may find yourself praying to Saint Nicholas to throw you a bag of gold coins!

Once you get to Demre, there is no shortage of tourist touts who offer guides and souvenirs. Though there isn't really that much to see, the town's splendid location makes up for this. Make your way to the Church of St. Nicholas, now re-named the Father Christmas Museum, for the most authentic experience. If you venture to Patara, all you will see are guesthouses and the vast, beautiful Patara Beach.

Idea for the Classroom: Pickled Onions Recipe

Pickled onions are traditionally eaten with fish and chips or a Ploughman's Lunch. They are stored in large jars on the shelves of Fish & Chip Shops in the UK. If you prepare the pickled onions in the autumn then they will be ready for Christmas and New Year. Our recipe does not involve cooking and will make three small (½ kg) jars of tasty pickled onions.

The onions will be ready to eat within a month or two. Once opened, keep refrigerated. They should last up to nine months and bring pleasure to all who eat them!

Ingredients

1kg pickling onions
2-3 tablespoons of pickling spices (or your own mix using coriander seeds, black peppercorns, and dried chilli flakes)
1 litre malt vinegar
(some recipes add salt and sugar to taste)

Preparation time: 30 minutes
Makes: three ½kg jars

Method

1. Peel the onions.
2. Fill up a ½kg jar about a third full with the onions.
3. Scatter a third of the pickling spices over the onions, then add another layer of onions, another of pickling spices and so on.
4. Pour the malt vinegar into the jar, covering all the onions. Make sure there are no air pockets.
5. Put the lid on the jar to seal it, and store it in a cool, dark place for one or two months.

Idea for the Classroom: Finger Puppets

Playing with finger puppets is an easy form of role-play, and children love to give their puppets characteristics of their own. It is often easier for a child to speak, act, or show emotions through the use of puppets. You can choose any theme you like for your finger puppets (animals, family members, pop stars); I have chosen a ballerina and robot for the template below.

Have a look on the internet and find pictures or line drawings – you can even find some ready-made puppet templates on the net. Get the children to colour and cut the character out, and then help them to attach a small strip of paper round the back of the character that the child can put over their finger. Use glue or tape for this.

Helping to make ten puppets for each child may be time consuming, so you might like to limit the number of puppets to one for each hand. But with a full hand of puppets your children can enjoy role-play and character development.

Idea for the Classroom: Christmas Decorations

At Christmas or New Year's it is wonderful to adorn the house or school with decorations. Why not try this simple paper decoration to make and hang from the ceiling or door frame?

Start with a square piece of paper of whatever size you like. Fold it in half and in half again and you should have a square a quarter of the original size (see the template below). Making sure that you start with the folded edges, cut 'L' shapes into the paper, first from the left, then from the right, then the left again and so on. Open out the paper into its original square shape, then lift or pull the centre of the square (the top of the decoration) and then all the other segments will follow. Stretch the segments out and you end up with a segmented lantern shape.

Finger Puppets

FINGER PUPPETS

ROBOT

BALLERINA

Christmas Decoration

CHRISTMAS DECORATION

folded edge

second cut

etc.

first cut

third cut

folded edge

BARRY NICHOLSON

4.
THE GREY
WOLF
LEGEND

4. THE GREY WOLF LEGEND

The Legend of the grey wolf Ashina (Asena) is an old Turkic myth that tells how the Turkic people were created.

The grey wolf is a common motif in many parts of the world, symbolising good luck, honour and the warrior. The wolf is a predator and symbolises danger and destruction, as portrayed in children's fairy tales such as *Little Red Riding Hood*.

Though called grey, the wolves can vary in colour including grey, white, brown, black and tan. They live in packs of up to eight, led by an alpha male. They are one of the most widespread land mammals and can be found in North America, Europe, Asia, and the very north-east of Africa, but their threat to survival comes from humans in the form of development, hunting, and loss of habitat.

Among the Turks and Mongols they are a revered animal and are considered to be the mother of Turkic people, who are said to be descended from wolves. In this respect the Turks apparently acquired some characteristics of the grey wolf such as courage, strength and agility; the wolf is largely seen as a good luck symbol, especially for males.

The tale goes that there was a small Turkic village in northern China of no more than a hundred dwellers. The village was raided by Chinese soldiers and only one young boy survived the battle. An old she-wolf with a sky-blue mane found the young boy and nursed him back to health. After impregnating the wolf, she gave birth to ten half-wolf half-human boys one of whom was named Ashina who went on to become the leader of the Ashina Clan and ruled the ancient Turks.

It is believed that the pregnant wolf escaped her enemies by crossing the Western Sea to a cave near the Qocho and Altai Mountain regions of western Siberia. Described as "a secret earthly paradise in the mountains", this land is quite a long geographical distance from modern-day Turkey. The 'Golden Mountains of Altai' are now a UNESCO World Heritage Site and consist steppe, mixed forest, and alpine vegetation, and provide habitat for endangered species such as the snow leopard. There is no particular reason to visit (and I haven't) unless the reader has ecological interest.

A better plan is to visit one of the large national parks in the USA or Canada to catch sight of the iconic animal, a place where the wolf is also revered. Yellowstone National Park has had a scheme in place to reintroduce grey wolves to the wild since 1995. Though controversial, the introduction of wolves caught in Canada has been very successful, and the wolves were down-listed from 'endangered' to 'threatened' by the US Fish and Wildlife service in 2003. If you happen to be in the area, the best place to see them is apparently the Lamar Valley between Mammoth and Cooke City where you can park your vehicle early in the morning and listen for their howl.

You are unlikely to catch a glimpse of the grey wolf in Turkey as they are few in number and very shy of contact with humans. Probably more interesting to visit in eastern Turkey are the cities of Kars and Van which have a wealth of historical and archaeological interest to the visitor in their vicinity (see the chapters on Akdamar Island, Van, and the deserted city of Ani). There are regular flights from Istanbul to both Kars and Van, from where an airport bus will whisk you to the centre of your chosen town.

Idea for the Classroom: Grey Wolf Jeopardy Quiz

This is a good way to learn and review the facts connected with the grey wolf and its habitat. The format copies the famous American TV show *Jeopardy*.

The quiz has five sections: Body, Pack, Geography, Spelling, and Pictures. Divide your students into teams and let them choose their category with 100 points awarded for a correct answer to an easy question, or 500 points awarded for a correct answer to the most difficult question. The team with the highest score wins! Start by drawing or projecting the game board and mark off each square with an "X" after it has been chosen (example below).

	100	200	300	400	500
body	X				
pack					X
geography		X			
spelling					
pictures					

Body

- 100 What colour is a grey wolf? (grey, white, brown, black, tan)
- 200 How tall is a grey wolf? (26-32 inches / 66-81cm)
- 300 How long is a grey wolf? (4½-6½ feet / 1.5 metres)
- 400 How fast can a grey wolf run? (up to 40 mph/64kmh)
- 500 How many teeth does a grey wolf have? (42)

Pack

- 100 What is the leader of the grey wolf pack called? (the alpha)
- 200 How many wolves live in a pack? (six to eight, typically)
- 300 What does a grey wolf eat? (elk, deer, moose, rabbit)
- 400 How many babies does a mother wolf have? (four to six, typically)
- 500 How many years does a grey wolf live? (up to thirteen years in the wild, up to sixteen years in captivity)

Geography

- 100 Where do grey wolves live? a) Turkey and Mongolia b) USA and Africa c) North America, Europe, Asia and Africa. (c)
- 200 In what park in the USA was the grey wolf re-introduced in 1995? (Yellowstone National Park)
- 300 Name three countries where grey wolf mythology is common. (Turkey, Mongolia, USA, Canada...)
- 400 How large is the territory of a grey wolf pack? (35km², on average)
- 500 What is the main threat to the grey wolf's survival? (humans – development, hunting, loss of habitat)

Spelling: How do you spell?

- 100 alpha
- 200 predator
- 300 mammal
- 400 Mongolia
- 500 mythology

Pictures

- 100 Who is this? (Ashina and the she-wolf)

- 200 What is the average foot size of the grey wolf? (4×5" or 10×12cm)

- 300 Can baby wolves see? (no, they are born blind)

- 400 Do grey wolves eat meat or vegetables? (meat: they are carnivores)

- 500 What noise does a grey wolf make? (howl!)

Idea for the Classroom: Wild Animals Poem

Think about some basic ways to describe animals – how many legs, fur, skin or scales, horns, mane, feet or trotters – as a way to introduce the idea of a wild animals poem. Ask questions: What is your favourite animal? What does it look like? Where does it live? What does it eat?

A simple animal poem involves describing just one animal and some of its characteristics as a gap-fill:

> I am a _lion_.
> I live in the _jungle_.
> I have _four_ legs.
> My fur is _yellow_.
> And I have a _short_ tail.
> Around my head I have a _mane_.
> What do I eat? I eat _meat_.
> And am I friendly? No, I'm _angry_.
> Don't come near me or I will _eat you_.
> Some of my _friends_ live in the zoo.

What about some other wild animals? You could try to construct a poem about them using adjectives:

> Lions are _____.
> Elephants are _____.
> Monkeys are _____.
> Fish are _____.
> Crocodiles are _____.
> Parrots are _____.
> Snakes are _____.
> Dolphins are _____.
> Giraffes are _____.
> And people are _____!

Another type of poem is an acrostic poem – the first letter of each line spells out a key word or phrase:

What's your favourite animal?
I think it's a hippo. No?
Let me guess...
Don't tell me!
Ape?
Newt?
Iguana?
Monkey?
Another animal?
Let me think...
Snake? Yes!

Idea for the Classroom: Grey Wolf Mask

A grey wolf is a wild animal that lives and hunts in packs. Create your own pack of wolves with this simple handicraft. Photocopy the template below, one for each student, and get them to colour and cut it out. You may have to help them cut out the eyes. Cut strips of paper and tape or glue them to the mask to make a head band. Alternatively, use string or elastic band. What a splendid little wolf pack! Howl!

Grey Wolf Mask

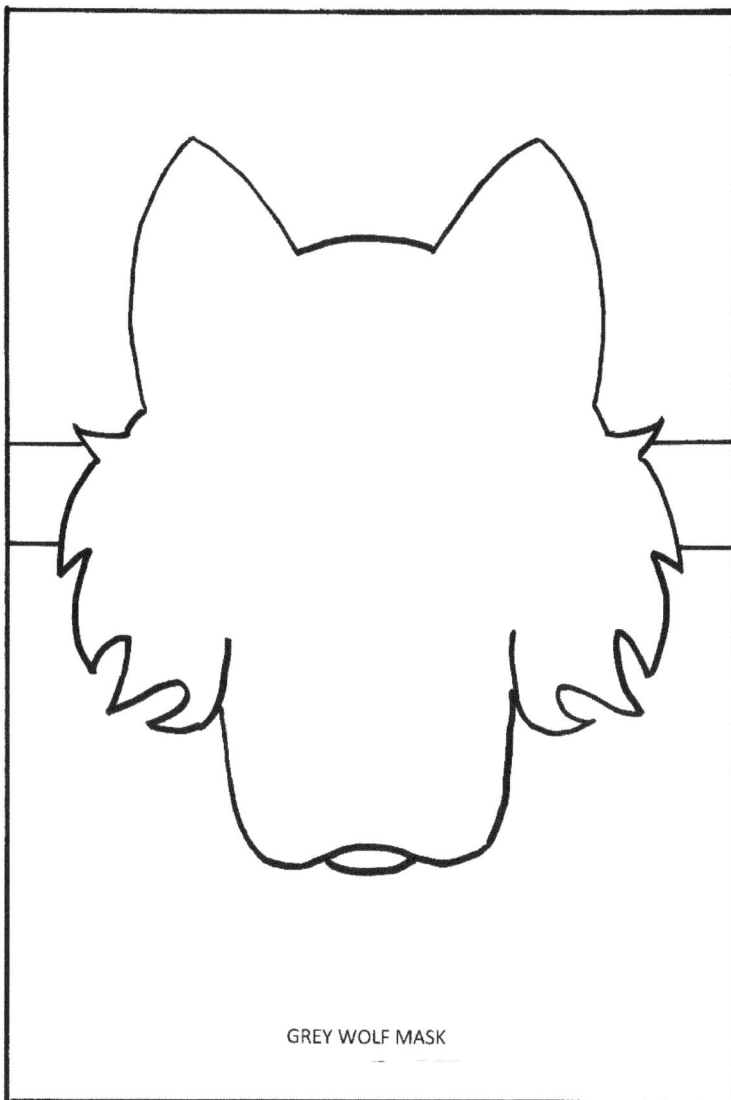

GREY WOLF MASK

5.
TURKISH
SKY DRAGONS

BARRY NICHOLSON

5. TURKISH SKY DRAGONS

Turkish Sky Dragons have a major symbolic role: they bring rain, prosperity and power. They live in the sky among the clouds above the Diyarbakir area of Turkey and also in the caves of the Karaca Mountains and Bitlis areas nearby.

The dragon is a frightening, supernatural figure, often stylised as snake-like. Some are winged, some breathe fire, some have seven heads, some have eyes that burn like a torch. In early Turk beliefs they carried positive traits as a symbol of plenty, fruitfulness, prosperity and strength. Later, under the influence of Arabs and Iranians, they were seen as frightening, harmful, and a symbol of evil. The Cambridge Dictionary Online defines a dragon as "a big, imaginary creature which breathes out fire".

But of course the dragon is an imaginary creature, isn't it?

Legend has it that an antelope became pregnant after seeing a bright star one autumn evening. While giving birth in the spring she noticed that one of the litter was born as a pouch and she kicked it with her back legs in fright. The baby in the pouch suddenly grew and became a dragon. Angels then descended from the heavens and took it up into the clouds.

According to the legend, dragons in the sky descend to the human world every autumn and spend the winter in a cave in the Karaca Mountains. During this time they feed once a day from a tail that descends from the sky. At the onset of spring the heavenly angels let down chains from the sky which the dragons use to get back into the clouds. Travellers have been known to stay in the caves with the dragons over the winter period, also feeding from this 'tail from the sky'. In spring the traveller takes hold of the tail and is able to get back to the surface safely.

In Turk cosmology there is a twelve animal calendar (similar to the Chinese Zodiac) and the animal in the calendar determines what the year will bring. The dragon is the fifth animal of the year and brings rain, prosperity and abundance. Country folk of the Diyarbakir area traditionally determine if the year will be prosperous or lean, conflicting or peaceful, based on the number of curls of the 'cloud dragon' that appears over the Karaca Mountains in the month of May.

The subject of dragons, and specifically Turkish dragons, is clearly fascinating; it is a product of people's imagination but has roots in reality.

What can today's traveller to the Diyarbakir area of south-west Turkey see of the dragons? Most commonly the dragon can be seen as a motif in Anatolian art, architecture, ceramics, carpets and weavings. There are tangible cultural products produced for tourists (gift items, books and guides, fridge magnets) and the intangible (such as festivals, music, excursions and tours).

Most prominent in tourist literature is the Mardin Dragon (Mardin lies south-east of Diyarbakir), and together with the Karaca Mountains these places form a 'dragon triangle'. Unfortunately I could find no evidence of dragon tours or stands of dragon memorabilia; much of the tourist activity is instead concentrated in the vicinity of nearby Mount Nemrut to the west.

There is some potential here to market the area as a 'dragon destination' and make use of this 'dragon triangle'. I have not visited the Karaca Mountains area, but I am sure there are caves to be found that can be billed as dragon's dens, and plentiful tourist items that can be manufactured. In this way the fiery-eyed monster can be brought more to the forefront of Turks' and tourists' minds.

What do you think? Would you feel safe spending winter in a cave with one of these sky dragons? Or is the whole idea a product of human imagination?

Idea for the Classroom: Paper Dragon

Turkish dragons are fantastic, but the most well-known dragon is the Chinese dragon – big and colourful, with a sweeping tale. You'll need the template below and a couple of wooden coffee stirrers to make this dragon.

First colour and cut out the template. Stick it together to make the dragon shape, and attach the two coffee stirrers to either end of the dragon. You might like to fold the dragon's body, concertina style.

Practice making your dragon dance and sweep from side to side. What noise does a dragon make?

Idea for the Classroom: Zodiac Signs

In the Chinese calendar there are twelve animals: rat, ox, tiger, rabbit, snake, horse, sheep, monkey, rooster, dog, pig and finally the dragon. Each animal has its own characteristics, and some say that humans have similar personalities to the animals. To find out which is your birth animal look at the chart below. For example, if you were born in 2006, your zodiac sign is a dog. Dogs are loyal, sociable and lively. Does this describe your friends?

Rat	1996	2008	2020
Ox	1997	2009	2021
Tiger	1998	2010	2022
Rabbit	1999	2011	2023
Dragon	2000	2012	2024
Snake	2001	2013	2025
Horse	2002	2014	2026
Sheep	2003	2015	2027
Monkey	2004	2016	2028
Rooster	2005	2017	2029
Dog	2006	2018	2030
Pig	2007	2019	2031

Animals and their characteristics:

Rat:
intelligent, adaptable, charming, artistic, sociable

Ox:
loyal, reliable, strong, steady, determined

Tiger:
enthusiastic, courageous, ambitious, confident

Rabbit:
trustworthy, modest, sincere, sociable

Dragon:
lucky, imaginative, artistic, spiritual

Snake:
organized, intelligent, elegant, decisive

Horse:
adaptable, loyal, adventurous, strong

Sheep:
crafty, elegant, charming, sensitive, calm

Monkey:
charming, lucky, adaptable, lively, smart

Rooster:
honest, energetic, intelligent, confident

Dog:
loyal, sociable, courageous, diligent, lively, smart

Pig:
honourable, determined, optimistic, sincere, sociable

Idea for the Classroom: Make a Magic Potion

With a magic potion you can do anything – at least in theory. Wizards, witches, and Harry Potter himself have all used magic potions for their various reasons, good and bad. Now you can mix a cocktail of your own and try it out on your friends.

All you need to start is a large cooking pot or saucepan. Your ingredients are coca-cola, lemonade (soda), orange juice, and cherry juice. Add the ingredients in equal parts into the cooking pot and stir. Chop up some fruit and stir it in. Use a ladle to spoon the potion into individual cups, and wait for the magical effects when you drink it.

Paper Dragon

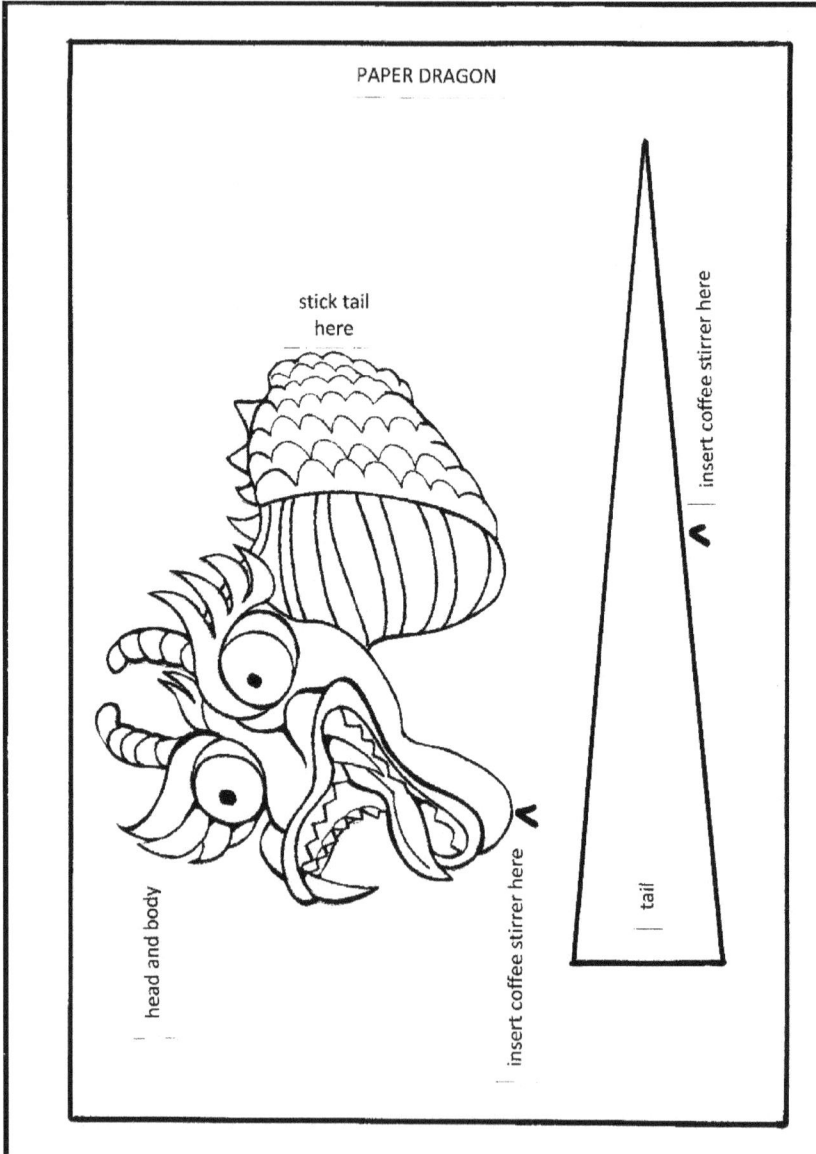

PAPER DRAGON

stick tail here

insert coffee stirrer here

head and body

insert coffee stirrer here

tail

6.
MAIDEN'S CASTLE, ISRANBUL

BARRY NICHOLSON

6. MAIDEN'S CASTLE, ISTANBUL

The story of Maiden's Castle shows that love in extreme can actually have a negative effect.

Within its life the castle has been a palace, a prison, a storage place, a lighthouse, and a quarantine hospital. These days it is an exclusive restaurant. The building is petit but well-formed: a small stone construction with a single turret, flag atop. The current stone structure was built by the architect Nevsehirli Damat Ibrahim Pasa after a fire destroyed the old wooden tower in 1719. A lead-covered dome was added later, a lantern was added to the tower in 1857, and in 1920 the light was converted into an electric automatic system. It was handed to the Ministry of Defence in 1964 and then to Maritime Enterprises in 1982.

The island holds a sad tale. There was once a Sultan who loved his daughter very much, but a fortune teller predicted that the princess would be killed by a snakebite. In order to protect his daughter he had a castle built on a small rocky outcrop in the Bosphorus, not far from the shores of modern Kadikoy.

Time passed and the princess grew up safely in the castle. One day the princess fell sick, but the doctors were wise and were able to find a remedy. To celebrate, the Sultan had many gifts sent to the tower. An old peasant woman brought a basket of grapes but unfortunately a poisonous snake was hiding inside. It slithered out and killed the princess in her sleep. The over-protective Sultan was left alone without a daughter – the fortune teller had been right after all.

Another sad tale is the love story of Hero and Leandros and gives the tower its other name – Leander's Tower. Hero was one of the priestesses of Aphrodite and love was forbidden for her. However, when attending a ceremony at the Temple of Aphrodite she met and fell in love with a young man, Leandros. Their secret love lasted for years as every night Hero built a fire in the tower so that Leandros could swim to meet his lover after dark. One night, the fire was put out by a storm and Leandros lost his way and was swept away by the waters of the Bosphorus. When Hero learned of this she could not carry on and threw herself into the dark waters and died. Sometimes a secret and forbidden love continues in heaven. Can you see how this tale is similar to the one at Akdamar Island?

Maiden's Castle has a fine site at the start of the Bosphorus, with extensive views over the waters and beyond to SultanAhmet and Topkapi Palace. You can see it fairly clearly if you take the public ferry from Eminonu to Kadikoy and look from the top deck. A pair of binoculars helps. If you'd like to visit the building itself close-up then the only option is to eat at the restaurant (and have a romantic dinner between two continents). Booking is advisable, and the restaurant's boat will pick you up from the Kadikoy shore. Dress nicely, and make sure your wallet or purse is well-charged.

Idea for the Classroom: Paper Snake

Get your children to decorate and colour an A4 piece of paper or take a piece of colour A4 paper. Cut off the corners so that the paper becomes an oval shape. From the outside, start to cut the paper into a strip of about one and a half centimetres and continue cutting, round and round, until you reach the middle which you can make into a snake's head (see the example below). Cut out a forked tongue shape and stick it on too. Hold the snake by its head and when you lift it up, a long spiral snake will appear. It can be very effective to use a large sheet of art paper to make the snake and decorate your classroom into a jungle.

Idea for the Classroom: 3D Castle

Why not make a large castle for the corner of your classroom or play area out of old cardboard boxes? You need a load of old cardboard (for example like they use to pack fridges and TVs in) and check that it is safe as there are often large sharp staples that were used to hold the box together.

Design your castle! The most basic shape is to have a low outer wall of about three by three metres and a tower in one of the corners, a metre or more high. The walls and tower need castle-tops that you might like to cut out yourself before class. The children's main job is to decorate the castle – windows and doors, people, a King and Queen, trees and flowers, birds and animals, and of course a flag on top of the tower.

The children love to play in the castle and you can make fancy dress costumes and a crown, or use the castle as a backdrop for a class play or presentation in assembly. As the castle is made of card, it can easily be folded away and used another time.

Idea for the Classroom: Maiden's Dress

You need a prince and princess for your castle, and it is very easy to dress your children for the part. To make your maiden's costume you need to start with a robe – a tablecloth or old curtain (white lacy curtains work well as they are light and easily washed). Drape the cloth or curtain around the princess and add a paper crown to her head. Princesses always have jewels, so make a necklace and bracelet out of yellow paper for gold, red and green for precious stones. A plastic rose completes the picture. Voila!

Your prince can be dressed a little differently. The crown is the same, but instead of a robe try to find an old waistcoat or jacket and decorate it with sparkly jewels. The prince needs a horse – either a hobby horse or broomstick.

For extra fun combine all three ideas above and have a castle complete with prince, princess and snakes, just like the real Maiden's Castle. What a great way to bring an old legend to life!

Paper Snake

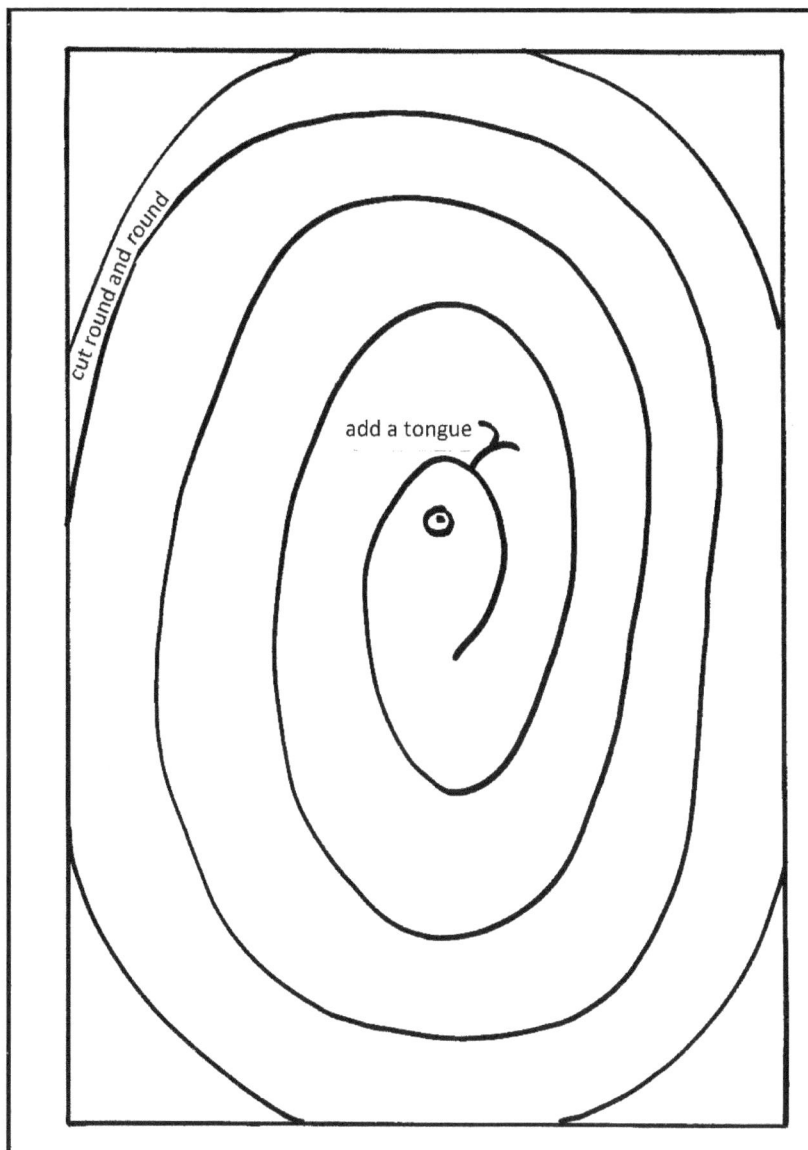

cut round and round

add a tongue

7.
AKDAMAR ISLAND, VAN

BARRY NICHOLSON

7. AKDAMAR ISLAND, VAN

Just like Romeo and Juliet, Akdamar Island has a lover's tale of its own. Is it possible to separate two hearts which are in love?

The island lies on Lake Van in eastern Turkey and although it is just under a kilometre in size, it is the home to the Armenian-built Church of the Holy Cross (Holy Cross Cathedral). The church is the sole survivor of an impressive complex of streets, gardens, terraced gardens, and a palace, constructed in the tenth century by King Gagik of Armenia. The pink volcanic rock of the fifteen metre long church melts into the backdrop of the clear blue waters of the lake and the surrounding snow-covered mountains.

The origin and meaning of the island's name is based on a tragic love story. An Armenian princess named Tamar fell in love with a commoner, Mehmet, and was banished to the island by her over-protective father. So deep was their love, however, that the young man would swim to the island each night guided by the princess's oil lamp that she had set on the rocks to guide him. Unfortunately her father found out about this and in anger smashed the oil lamp to pieces. Of course, now the boy did not know which way to swim, became lost, and drowned as he hit some dangerous rocks. Princess Tamar was so distraught that she too threw herself into the waters and drowned. According to the tale, his body washed ashore and it appeared as if the words "Akh, Tamar" ("Oh, Tamar") were frozen on his lips. If you visit at night you can still hear the boy's dying cries of "Akh, Tamar" which give the island its name.

There are no princesses or palaces these days, however the site is well worth a visit. The church is most impressive. Standing 20.4 metres high, it is cross-shaped with a central dome. It underwent extensive restoration in 2005-2006, apparently as a peace offering to the Armenian community by the Turkish government to ease their tense relations. The church was turned into a museum and opened in 2007, and a religious ceremony has been held here every year since 2010.

Of particular importance are the magnificent stone reliefs on the outside walls of the church, carved by Armenian master carvers. There are two main themes to the reliefs. First, religious Biblical scenes: Jonah about to be swallowed by the whale, Adam and Eve, David and Goliath, and King Gagik presenting a miniature of his church to Christ. Second, scenes of animals, palace life, and hunting. They combine to form a work of art set in stone, with detail unusual and unique in Armenian architecture.

Once you have soaked up the architecture and atmosphere, hike up the steep hill behind the church for breath-taking views across the church and lake to the mountains beyond. If you have time, take a swim at the bathing spot near the landing stage. Surprisingly, it is a salt water lake at an elevation of 1,670 metres so swimming is very easy. How Lake Van and other lakes in the area came to be salt lakes is a mystery.

The setting is most impressive in late spring when the island is covered with a colourful bloom, though the best temperatures are in the summer and early autumn. Put your mind to it and you can imagine King Gagik's palace and gardens surrounding the church.

To get to Akdamar Island your starting point is the eastern city of Van, from where you can locate a dolmus (minibus) to the ferry pier near the town of Gevas (your driver should know where to drop you off). Boats seat ten to twelve people and set off on the twenty minute journey when full. Walk around at your leisure as the boat will wait until the last passenger arrives for the return journey.

Idea for the Classroom: Lover's Lantern

Princess Tamar used an oil lamp to guide her lover safely to the shore, and you too can make a decorative lamp out of paper.

Start with a piece of colourful A4 paper (or whatever size you like) and fold it in two lengthways. With scissors, cut slits on the folded edge at 45 degrees, at about one centimetre intervals, as shown in the template below. When this is done, open the paper and put the two shorter ends together and press out the strips so that they protrude outwards. Stick the two short ends together with tape or glue. Add a handle across the top of the lamp using a thin strip of paper. Make a number of these in various colours and sizes to decorate your classroom or corridor.

Idea for the Classroom: Hearts Mobile

Another idea to decorate your classroom is to make a hearts mobile. Draw and cut out some heart templates of different sizes for the children to use, like the examples below. They can select a template and use it as a stencil to draw out heart shapes on colourful paper, then cut them out carefully using scissors. Find some cheap coat-hangers and string so that the children can hang their hearts in decorative style. Alternatively hang the hearts around the classroom singly, or make badges out of the hearts for the children to stick on their tummy.

Idea for the Classroom: Princess Tiara

Every young girl wants to dress as a princess and the easiest way is to make a tiara, bracelet and necklace.

To make the tiara, cut out a strip of paper long enough to fit over the child's head and stick it together to make a simple head band. The fun part is to decorate it with cut-out hearts, stars and other shapes that can be stuck on with glue (see below). A bracelet can be made in a similar way but smaller, again with hearts and other shapes stuck on. The necklace is a little different as you use string instead of paper, and attach diamonds and hearts to the string. Do you think this jewellery is enough to attract a prince?

Lover's Lantern Template

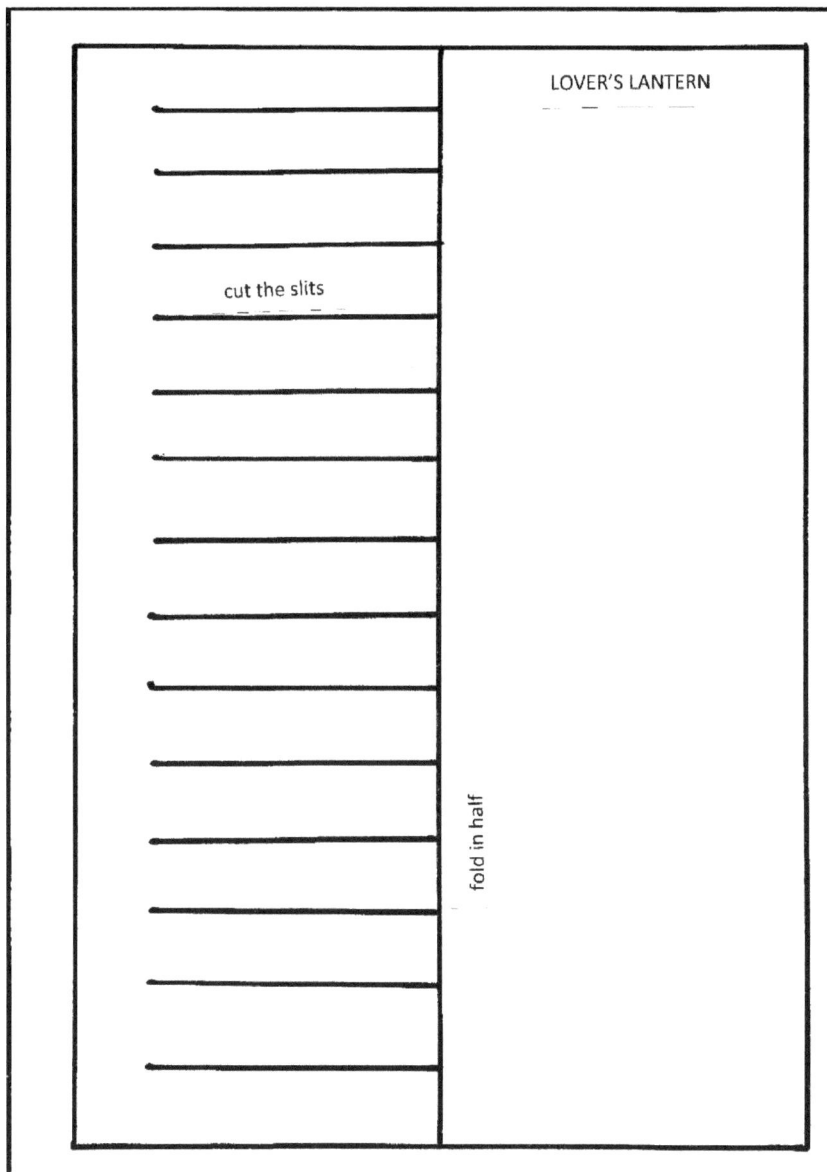

LOVER'S LANTERN

cut the slits

fold in half

Hearts Mobile / Princess Tiara

HEARTS

8.
THE DESERTED
GHOST CITY
OF ANI

BARRY NICHOLSON

8. THE DESERTED GHOST CITY OF ANI

Some cities are alive, others fade away into history and lie in ruins for the adventurous to explore.

Deserted cities have an air of mystery and wonder about them; we wonder who used to live there, how they came to be abandoned, and admire the ruins that they have become. No deserted city is quite like that of Ani in eastern Turkey, and a visit there confirms that the photos are as spooky as they seem: pinkish stone ruins on a desolate grassy landscape. It is an unfortunate place, sandwiched between modern day Turkey and the neighbouring country of Armenia. Indeed, it is an Armenian city and is now only in Turkey by default. What one makes of the attempts to restore parts of the city is a matter of opinion, but the scattered buildings that remain are sure to stick in anyone's mind.

There has been settlement in Ani for the last 1,600 years, but its main claim to fame was as a staging post on the Silk Road. Ani controlled trade routes between Byzantium, Persia, Syria, central Asia and beyond. It became a walled city of over 100,000 people and capital of the Armenian Empire under the Bagratid Dynasty. As more and more merchants, craftsmen and farmers flocked to the city it became known as "the city of a thousand and one churches" and "the city of forty gates".

But this was not to last. Mongol invasions led to mass emigration from the city and by the fourteenth century the trade routes had moved south. Some say Ani was further abandoned after an earthquake in 1319. The region became over-run by unruly nomadic Kurdish tribes and by the mid nineteenth century the site was totally abandoned.

Ani enjoyed a brief moment of fame in the late nineteenth century as the number of European travellers gradually increased and, under Russian archaeologist Nikolai Marr, the first archaeological excavations took place in 1892. City walls were uncovered, church frescos were revealed, and two museums were established... until World War 1 put an end to it.

Ani's neglect has not been helped by other factors, and damage to the site over the years can be divided into damage by natural events (such as earthquakes), damage by extreme weather, vandalism and looting, damage by the activities of archaeologists, and questionable attempts at restoration.

Still, there is much to interest the visitor. Most accounts of Ani focus on the churches and cathedral (which has recently been restored), but I find the city gates and their walls more interesting. The strongest defences were built on Ani's northern side: a line of double walls consisting of a dry moat, lower outer wall, and a much higher inner wall with numerous semi-circular towers, in places decorated with patterns or symbols.

There are three main gates on the northern side. The Chequerboard Gate has a panel of red and black stone squares over its entrance giving the gate its name. The Lion Gate takes its name from a relief of a lion on a nearby wall and was probably the main entrance to Ani (a street ran from here to the centre of the city). The gate has twin towers, the one on the left being well-preserved. Finally the Kars Gate has large towers on either side, each with a complex of rooms. Between the gates the wall is an impressive line of fortifications and towers.

Ani has become an area of increased tourist interest in recent years, despite the tense border between Turkey and Armenia. Photography restrictions have recently been lifted, and anyone can now visit the site without permission. It is a large and open site, with sloping hills, cliffs and rocky valleys, exposed to the elements. Parts are sometimes off limits, but if it is accessible the best views are from the fortress.

Getting to Ani can be troublesome; it is impossible to visit in winter when the site is snowed in, and it is best to visit in June when the hills are covered with wild flowers. Your starting point is Kars in eastern Turkey where you have two options. Either hire a taxi for the day that will earn you a five-hour trip with three hours on site, or go by private car and follow the well-surfaced highway that connects Kars with Ani. Whatever you do, bring a packed lunch and water as there are no facilities.

As I write this (April 2015) there is an article in the Hürriyet Daily News about the Turkish government's plans to restore many buildings of Armenian origin throughout Turkey. It's good news because a lot of the buildings need intensive care. So, what will happen to Ani? Will attempts at restoration be successful? I hope so, not so much because it will lessen the Turkish-Armenia ill-feeling, but more because beautiful architecture of historical importance will be preserved.

Idea for the Classroom: Chequerboard Mosaic

Making a Chess or Drafts board is relatively easy – all you need are some black square shapes that can be stuck on to a square of white paper. Cut out circles for the Drafts pieces, or draw and cut out Chess pieces for a full chess set. You can use the grid below or make one of your own. More creative is to make a Chequerboard Gate in 2D or in 3D out of cardboard and colourful paper squares, perhaps using the gate template below.

Chequerboard Gate

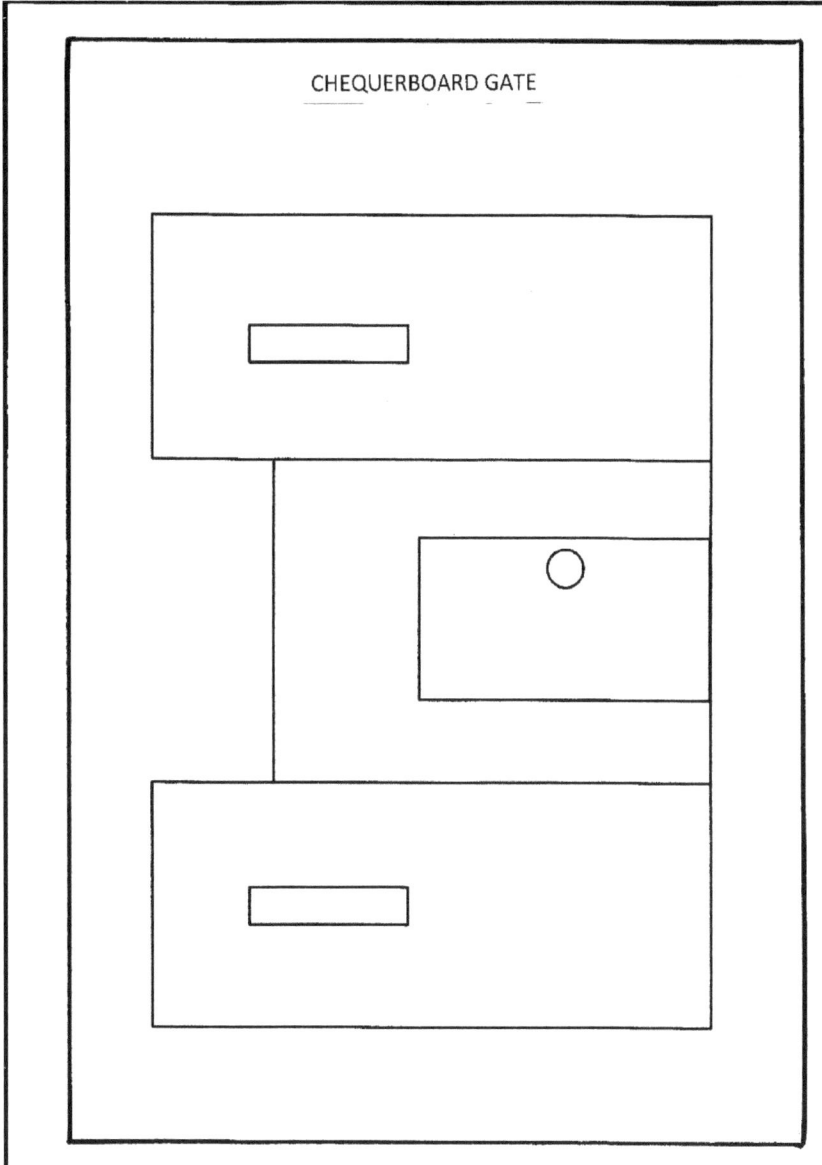

CHEQUERBOARD GATE

Idea for the Classroom: Turkey's Neighbours: Did You Know?

Turkey has land borders with eight countries, fourteen if you count countries the other side of seas, and Cyprus. But did you know these interesting facts about Turkey and its neighbours?

Turkey
Capital: Ankara
Land area: 783,562km²
Population: 77,695,904 (2014)
Currency: Turkish Lira
Interesting fact: The modern state of Turkey was founded by Mustafa Kemal Ataturk in 1923.

Greece (land border 206km)
Capital: Athens
Land area: 131,957km²
Population: 10,815,197 (2012)
Currency: Euro
Interesting fact: The most famous historic building in Athens is the Parthenon, overlooking the city. Construction began in 447BC, and it is dedicated to the goddess Athena.

Bulgaria (land border 240km)
Capital: Sofia
Land area: 110,994km²
Population: 7,364,570 (2011)
Currency: Lev
Interesting fact: Bulgaria's biggest ski resorts are Bansko, Pamporovo and Borovets, and the best coastal resorts are Golden Sands and Sunny Beach.

Romania (no land border)
Capital: Bucharest

Land area: 238,391km²
Population: 19,942,642 (2014)
Currency: Leu
Interesting fact: Dracula comes from Transylvania in modern day
Romania. The main tourist attraction is Bran Castle, also known as
Dracula's Castle.

Russia (no land border)
Capital: Moscow
Land area: 17,098,242km²
Population: 143,975,923 (2015)
Currency: Ruble
Interesting fact: Russia is the largest country in the world, and its
largest constituent is Siberia at 13.1 million km². Siberia covers
77% of the land area, but has just 27% of the population.

Ukraine (no land border)
Capital: Kiev
Land area: 603,500km²
Population: 44,291,413 (2014)
Currency: Hryvnia
Interesting fact: Chicken Kiev takes its name from the place.
Introduced to the UK in 1976, it was Marks and Spencer's first
ready-made meal.

Georgia (land border 252km)
Capital: Tblisi
Land area: 69,700km²
Population: 3,729,500 (2015)
Currency: Lari
Interesting fact: The Georgian flag consists a white background
with a red cross (placed horizontally and vertically), and each
white compartment has a smaller red cross.

Armenia (land border 268km)
Capital: Yerevan

Land area: 29,743km²
Population: 3,018,854 (2011)
Currency: Dram
Interesting fact: The largest Armenian population in Turkey is in Istanbul, with around 70,000 people.

Azerbaijan (land border 9km)
Capital: Baku
Land area: 86,600km²
Population: 9,494,600 (2014)
Currency: Manat
Interesting fact: Won the Eurovision Song Contest in 2011 with 'Running Scared' by Ell and Nikki. The contest that year was staged in Dusseldorf, Germany.

Iraq (land border 331km)
Capital: Baghdad
Land area: 437,072km²
Population: 36,004,552 (2014)
Currency: Dinar
Interesting fact: The former leader was Saddam Hussein, who was toppled in the 2003 invasion led by the US. The war officially ended in 2011.

Iran (land border 499km)
Capital: Tehran
Land area: 1,648,195km²
Population: 78,192,200 (2013)
Currency: Rial
Interesting fact: Tehran's first two metro lines were opened in 2001; now there are five lines, totalling 152km.

Syria (land border 822km)
Capital: Damascus
Land area: 185,180km²
Population: 17,951,639 (2014)

Currency: Syrian Pound
Interesting fact: In 539BC the Persians took Syria as part of their empire, and later it was part of the Seleucid Empire whose capital was Antioch, just inside the Turkish border today.

Egypt (no land border)
Capital: Cairo
Land area: 1,010,407km²
Population: 88,984,000 (2015)
Currency: Egyptian Pound
Interesting fact: Howard Carter discovered Tutankhamun's tomb in the Valley of the Kings in 1922. It was filled with golden treasure, but was also home to a curse.

Libya (no land border)
Capital: Tripoli
Land area: 1,759,541km²
Population: 6,244,174 (2014)
Currency: Dinar
Interesting fact: The Libyan Desert, at 1,100,000km², is part of the Sahara Desert. It is one of the driest and sunniest places on earth and is famous for its naturally-formed Libyan Desert Glass.

Cyprus (land border?)
Capital: Nicosia
Land area: 9,251km²
Population: 1,141,166 (2013)
Currency: Euro
Interesting fact: Cyprus is an island country in the Eastern Mediterranean and member state of the EU. 59% of it is Greek, 36% Turkish-administered, and 5% British Overseas Territory.

Idea for the Classroom: Dried Flowers Bookmark

In late spring Ani's rolling slopes are covered with a mosaic of colourful wild flowers, and they are the inspiration for making a dried flower bookmark.

First you'll need to find some flowers, preferably wild flowers as they are rather pretty and can be pressed relatively flat; alternatively, try using the paper flower templates below. There are two ways to get the flowers ready to be put into your bookmark. A first way is to hang your bunch of wild flowers in a cool, dark place until they are dry – a process that can take several months. The second (and better) way is to press the flowers underneath some heavy books or bricks. This only takes about a week, and has the advantage that the flowers will keep most of their colour.

When the flowers are ready, arrange them decoratively on a piece of coloured paper or card that has been cut to bookmark size. Either place them on as a simple floral display, or make shapes or faces out of them. Experiment, as you may need to stick the flowers down with a tiny dab of glue. Next comes the tricky part – to laminate the bookmark. If your school does not have a laminating machine then probably your local photocopy shop will. After lamination, cut the bookmark out to its correct size and start to use in your book.

Paper Flower Templates

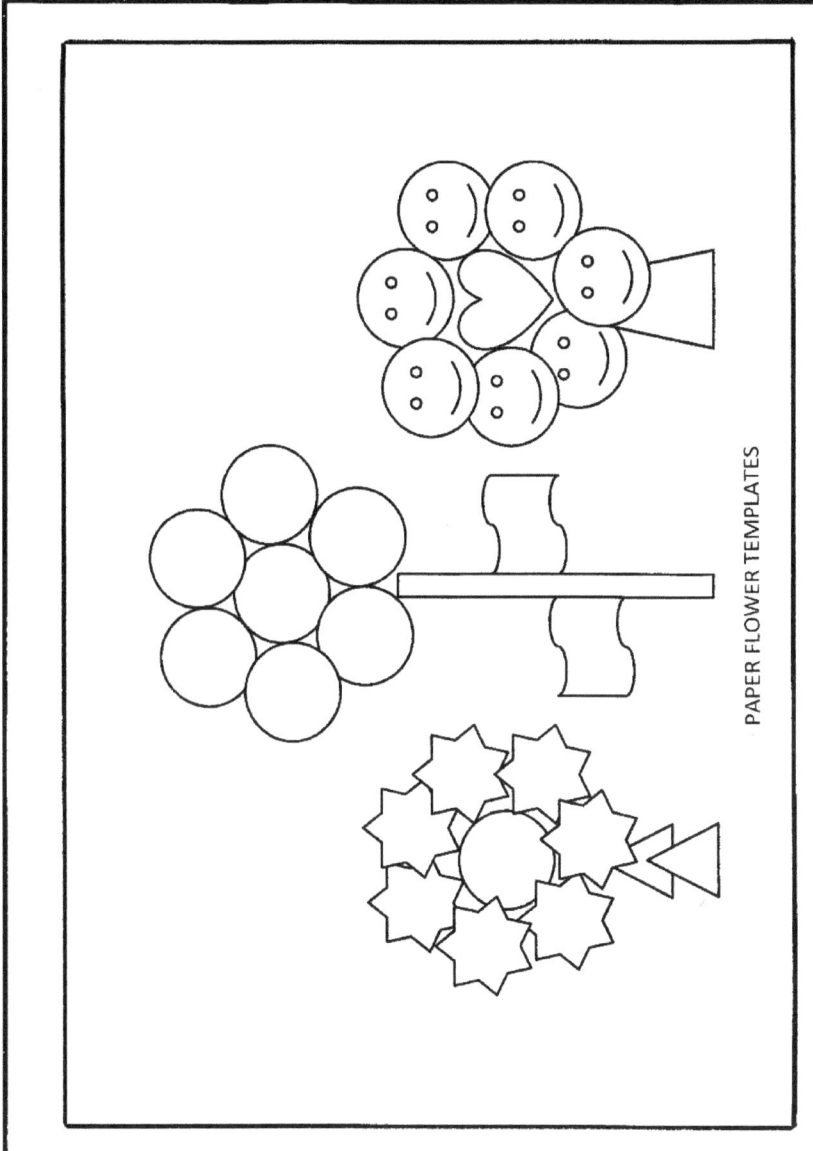

PAPER FLOWER TEMPLATES

9.
MOUNT NEMRUT'S STATUES OF THE PAST

9. MOUNT NEMRUT'S STATUES OF THE PAST

As royal tombs go, the constructions at Mount Nemrut are spectacular, not only for their size but also for their stunning location.

Mount Nemrut is a 2,134 metre-high mountain in south-east Turkey, and is famous because in 62 BC King Antiochus I Theos of Commagene built upon it a splendid tomb-sanctuary for himself surrounded by huge statues. The site embodies the ambition of a dynasty that sought to be independent of both East and West, and stands as one of the most unique and ambitious constructions of the Hellenistic period. The structures have survived to modern day in a reasonably well-preserved state and have become a symbol of modern Turkey.

The site was discovered by chance in 1881 by the German engineer Karl Sester who was assessing transport routes for the Ottomans. It was not until 1953 that exploration of the area began, and finally in 1987 the site was declared a World Heritage Site by UNESCO.

Mount Nemrut's main features are the giant tumulus (diameter 145 metres, height 50 metres) and three surrounding terraces. The conical tumulus, aswell as being ceremonial, also protected the tomb underneath from robbers. The interior layout remains unknown, and excavations have failed to find the tomb of Antiochus, somewhere in the mound. It is approached by a ceremonial road.

The east and west terraces are very similar to each other and consist of five giant limestone statues that face away from the tumulus, flanked by a lion and eagle pair. The statues represent various Greek, Armenian and Persian gods, the tallest of which stands at seven metres. Unfortunately the heads of the statues have fallen onto a lower terrace and are notably damaged. The only difference in design between the east and west terraces is the east terrace has a square altar while the west terrace has a temple. The third, north terrace, is eighty metres long, narrow and rectangular. It was probably used for processions or assemblies.

Though the structures are largely intact, weathering has taken its toll. Seasonal and daily temperature variations, freezing and thawing, wind, snow and sun exposure have all had their impact.

If you want to attempt a visit to Mount Nemrut, it is located between the modern cities of Malatya and Kahta, and from these two cities it is possible to take an overnight tour. More convenient is the nearby town of Adiyaman, from which car and bus trips to the site can be arranged. In 2009 two visitor centres were planned, on the roads to Malatya and Adiyaman: a useful source of information if they are open when you visit. Bear in mind that Mount Nemrut can only be visited in summer months because at other times it is snowed in.

Idea for the Classroom: Nemrut: Written Questions

Part 1: Answer the questions.

- What king ordered the structures at Mount Nemrut to be built?
- Who discovered the site in 1881?
- How high is Mount Nemrut?
- What two animals flank the east and west terraces?

Part 2: Complete the sentences.

- The tumulus has a height of _____.
- The north terrace was probably used for _____.
- You can visit Mount Nemrut from the cities of _____.
- Some of the statues have eroded due to _____.

Part 3: Order the words to make sentences.

- Turkey / Mount / Nemrut / symbol / modern / of / is / a
- 1987 / it / World / Heritage / a / became / Site / in
- statues / gods / Greek / Armenian / Persian / are / and / the
- Commagene / King / of / I / Theos / Antiochus

Part 4: Free writing.

Imagine you are Karl Sester, and you have just discovered the site. Describe what you see and how you feel. Start with this sentence:

"It was amazing. Today we found a wonderful place _____."

Answers
Part 1: King Antiochus I Theos of Commagene; Karl Sester; 2,134 metres; lion and eagle.
Part 2: fifty metres; processions and assemblies; Malatya, Kahta, and the town of Adiyaman; weathering.
Part 3: Mount Nemrut is a symbol of modern Turkey; It became a World Heritage Site in 1987; The statues are Greek, Armenian and Persian gods; King Antiochus I Theos of Commagene.

Idea for the Classroom: Paper Snowflakes

Nemrut can only be visited in the warmer months; in winter it is snowed in. How about making some snowflakes to decorate your walls or desk, or to complement a class project on Nemrut? Here's how.

Get a square piece of paper (it doesn't have to be big). Fold it in half, and in half again. Cut shapes such as triangles, rectangular slits, or half-moon shapes into the edges of the folded paper, but don't go overboard. Look at the example below. When you unfold the paper a beautiful snowflake will be revealed.

Idea for the Classroom: Comparatives and Superlatives Quiz

Divide the class into two or more teams. Ask the questions one by one, team by team, awarding a point for each correct answer.

COMPARATIVES AND SUPERLATIVES QUIZ

1. Easy

What's the highest mountain in the world? (Mount Everest)
What's the fastest animal in the world? (the cheetah)
What's the longest river in the world? (the Nile)

What's the biggest country in the world? (Russia)
What's the tallest animal in the world? (the giraffe)

2. So-So

What's the largest desert in Asia, the Great Indian Desert or the Gobi Desert? (the Gobi desert)
Which is the largest city in North America, Los Angeles or Mexico City? (Mexico City)
What is the deepest ocean in the world, the Atlantic or the Pacific? (the Pacific)
Which animal lives the longest, the whale, the elephant, or the tortoise? (the tortoise)
Which measurement is the longest, the yard, the kilometre, or the mile? (the mile)

3. Difficult

Which mountain is higher, Mount Kilimanjaro in Africa or Mount McKinley in Alaska? *Mount McKinley is higher than Mount Kilimanjaro.*

Which waterfall is higher, the Angel Falls in Venezuela or the Tugela Falls in South Africa? *The Angel falls are higher than the Tugela Falls.*

Where is the largest art gallery in the world, Italy, Spain or Russia? *The largest art gallery in the world is in Russia: the Winter Palace in St. Petersburg.*

What is the smallest country in the world, Monaco or the Vatican City? *The Vatican City is the smallest country in the world.*

What is the largest island in the world, Greenland or Australia? *Greenland is the largest island in the world.*

4. True or False?

Toe nails grow faster than finger nails. True or false?
False. Finger nails grow faster than toe nails.

Penguins can swim faster than humans. True or false?
True. They can swim four times faster than humans.

The largest animal is the African elephant. True or false?
False. The largest animal is the blue whale.

The largest active volcano in the world is in Hawaii. True or false?
True. The largest active volcano is Mauna Loa in Hawaii.

La Paz in Bolivia is the highest capital city in the world. True or false?
True. It is about 12,000 feet above sea level.

Paper snowflake template

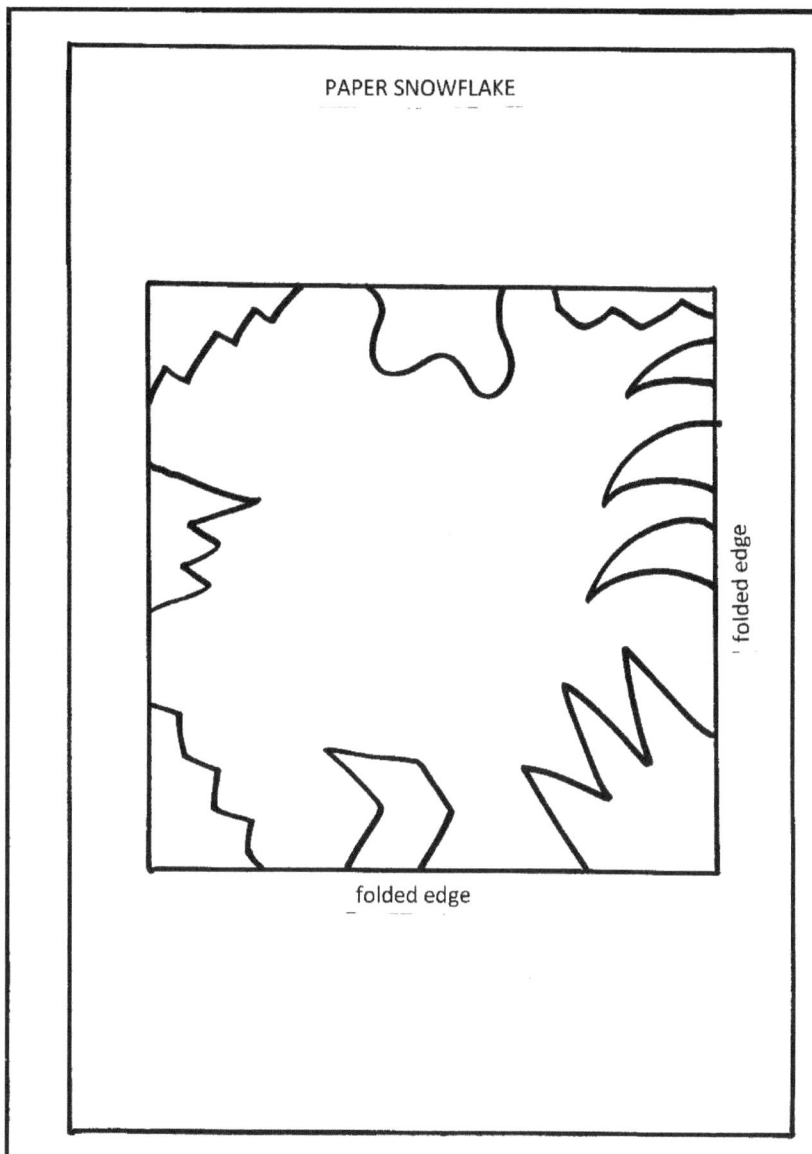

PAPER SNOWFLAKE

folded edge

folded edge

10.
NOAH'S ARK,
MOUNT ARARAT

BARRY NICHOLSON

10. NOAH'S ARK, MOUNT ARARAT

When Noah built an ark to escape the floods, it settled on Mount Ararat in Eastern Turkey.

Mount Ararat is located in Agri Province in eastern Turkey, near the borders with Iran, Armenia and Azerbaijan. It rises to a height of 5,137 metres (16,854 feet). In fact, it is the highest mountain in Turkey, although it is only the forty-eighth highest in the world.

The story of Noah's Ark is well-known, with origins in the Bible, and I start now with a summary. God was not pleased with all the greed and crime on earth so He decided the only way to solve the problem was to destroy the earth with a severe flood. He chose Noah and his family to survive the flood, and told Noah to build a large wooden ship (an ark) that would house his family and two of every kind of animal. Of course, all the other people laughed at him, and said he was stupid to build the ark.

Noah and his family, and the animals two by two, entered the ark. Then it began to rain. It rained for forty days and forty nights, and the earth was destroyed except for those in the ark.

After one hundred and fifty days Noah sent out a dove to try to find land. When the dove came back with an olive branch Noah knew there was dry land nearby. Indeed, soon after he found dry land and Noah and his family, and all the animals two by two, left the ark to start a new life.

In the Bible, the story of Noah's Ark appears in chapters six to nine of the Book of Genesis. Apparently the ark was built from gopher wood but in reality it was probably built from cypress wood. It measured "three hundred cubits" long, "fifty cubits" wide, and was "thirty cubits" high. One cubit is forty-eight point two centimetres, so the measurement translated into metres is 144 by 24 by 14.5 metres. The ark was capable of floating with as many as 70,000 animals on board according to a study by the Department of Physics and Astronomy, Leicester University. Using the ark's dimensions, the Archimedes principal of water displacement, and approximate weights of the animals, the team were amazed to find out that the ark would have floated (reported in *The Telegraph*, 3rd April 2014).

Several researchers have claimed to have found the ark, but the Mount Ararat area is not amenable to archaeological study. Firstly, the landscape itself is rather inhospitable; secondly it is near the tense border with Armenia. From a search of the internet I was able to find two published articles with claims to have found the ark, and although they are both claims by fundamental Christians, they give us plenty of food for thought.

The first article appeared in the *Daily Mail* (28th April 2010) under the title "We've Found Noah's Ark" and features some unlikely photos of the well-preserved interior of the wooden 'ark'. The team of fifteen Hong Kong and Turkish explorers say they found seven large wooden compartments beneath snow and volcanic debris close to the summit of Mount Ararat. They claim it is built with plank-like timber, of cypress wood, each about eight inches wide, and that samples taken from the site date from 2,800 BC.

Their video evidence included shots of smooth, curved walls, doors, and staircases.

Scientists remain sceptical about this "discovery", and even one of the team was quoted as saying "it's not one hundred percent that this is Noah's Ark, but we think it is 99.9 percent that this is it".

More believable is the evidence put forward in the article titled "Noah's Ark has been found. Why are they keeping us in the dark?" (sunnyskyz.com, December 13th 2013). It gives some historical background into Noah's Ark "discoveries" presented in a scientific and persuasive way.

It relates that the history of the site started in 1959 when Captain Durupinar of the Turkish army discovered an unusual shape while examining aerial photographs of the area: the shape stood out from the rocky terrain surrounding it. He sent the aerial photo to an expert at Ohio State University who concluded that the object was a ship beyond any doubt. In 1960 a group of Americans led by Captain Durupinar researched the site for two days looking for artefacts or remains. But they found nothing and concluded it was a natural formation.

Nothing more happened until 1977 when Ron Wyatt and his team started to study the site of the ark using more scientific methods (metal detectors, subsurface radar scans, and chemical analysis). They found the distance from bow to stern was 515 feet (300 cubits) and that all of the wood had been petrified. The symmetry and logical placement of the structure pointed towards a man-made object. The team discovered artefacts from within the ark such as petrified animal dung, a petrified antler, a length of cat hair, and nails and rivets far in advance of their time.

Academics are quick to pour scorn on such discoveries, saying that the expeditions are yet to produce compelling evidence and have underlying religious motivation. Is this really the site of Noah's Ark? Time will tell.

I think the academics are right to study Noah's Ark from the desk and armchair, as there is precious little for the visitor to the area to see. There are no 'ark attractions', souvenir stalls or visitor centres. The best you will find is brief mention in the region's tourist brochures. It is a shame, as so much more could be made of the location and its connection to this famous tale from Turkey.

Idea for the Classroom: Noah's Pudding Recipe

Facing starvation after many days in the ark, Noah gathered all the food they had and mixed it together to make a delicious dish called 'Noah's Pudding'. It consists wheat, rice, nuts, dried fruit and raisins and is not unlike museli. All the ingredients are boiled together to make a porridge that is served cold. The pudding is made at home and is shared with neighbours and the poor. The following recipe produces thirty servings.

Ingredients

1 cup wheat
1 cup white beans
1 cup garbanzo beans or rice
1 cup raisins
1 cup almonds
¾ cup peanuts
1 or 2 dried apricots
½ cup sugary water
walnuts and cinnamon to top

Preparation time: 30 minutes (plus overnight soak)
Makes: 30 small servings

Method

1. Soak wheat, beans and almonds overnight.
2. Boil these and remove the skins.
3. Boil the raisins in water until they soften.
4. Put all of the above ingredients into a large pot and boil. Crush the peanuts and almonds and add them at this point.
5. Chop the apricot into pieces and add to the mixture along with sugary water.
6. Boil for 10-15 minutes.

After the mixture has been left to cool, it is ready to eat. There are alternative ingredients, for example the addition of pomegranate or orange peel. As you eat, imagine yourself with Noah and his family and all the animals on the ark!

Idea for the Classroom: Animal Collage

Children love animals! Why not brighten up your classroom or corridor walls with a colourful animal collage?

Prepare the children by showing them pictures of various animals using flashcards, a book, or the interactive whiteboard. What does it look like? How big is it? How many legs does it have? How long is its tail? What's your favourite animal?

Give each child an A4 paper and get them to draw and colour their favourite animal. Tell them that they will cut their animal out (you can help them with this) and stick it onto a class collage. Have ready a large sheet of coloured paper and either stick it to the board or put it on a table at the front of the class. You might want to draw some basic tree or leaf shapes onto the paper. When the children have cut out their animal they can come to the front and, with your help, stick their artwork onto the big paper. Hey presto! You've got yourselves a scene from the jungle!

Idea for the Classroom: Noah's Ark Play

The story of Noah's Ark is good to be performed as a play as it uses distinct visual imagery (ark, animals, water, mountain) and involves a lot of characters including people and animals. Preparation for your performance could involve making the stage set: different animals, rain clouds, and the ark itself.

Characters

Narrator
Noah
Noah's Wife
Noah's Family (son and daughter)
God
Bad Person 1
Bad Person 2
Bad Person 3
Dove
Monkeys
Elephants
Lions
Snakes

Situation

A bare, rocky mountain in eastern Turkey, with some small towns and settlements. Vegetation is mostly palm trees and scrub.

Script

Bad Person 1: I am a bad person. I will steal your money.
Bad person 2: I am a bad person. I will fight with your friends.

Bad Person 3: I am a bad person. I will hit you and pull your hair.
God: Oh my goodness! Look at all the bad people. What shall I do?
(He thinks)
I know. I will send a great flood and kill all the bad people. But
there is one good man called Noah. I will save him and his family.

Narrator: Noah and his family are working in a field.

Noah: This is hard work.
Noah's Wife: Yes, we work so hard. We are good people.
Son: Can I take a rest?
Daughter: I'm hungry!
God: Noah! Noah! Can you hear me? I am God. I will send a great
flood. Build an ark. Take your family and animals two by two into
the ark and you will be safe.
Noah: What? An ark? OK, let's build it.

Narrator: Noah builds an ark.

Bad Person 1: You are so stupid!
Bad Person 2: What are you doing?
Bad Person 3: I don't believe it!
Noah: I am building an ark. A big flood will come. I will save my
family and animals from the flood.
Bad Person 1: Big flood? What a joke!
Bad People *(all)*: Ha Ha Ha!

Narrator: The animals board the ark two by two.

Monkeys: We are monkeys. We will be safe in the ark.
Elephants: We are elephants. We will be safe in the ark.
Lions: We are lions. We will be safe in the ark.
Snakes: We are snakes. We will be safe in the ark.

Bad Person 1: Look! It's raining!
Bad Person 2: Look! It's flooding!

Bad Person 3: Noah was right. We are drowning!
Bad People *(all)*: Ahhhhh!

Narrator: It rained for forty days and forty nights.

Noah: We are safe in the ark.
Noah's wife: Let's send out a dove to find land.
Noah: Good idea.
Dove: I will find land.
(the dove finds an olive branch)
Dove: Look! I have found an olive branch.
Noah: Yes, there must be land.

Narrator: A few days later the ark came to rest on land.

Son: We are safe!
Daughter: The water has gone!
Monkeys: We are safe!
Elephants: We are safe!
Lions: We are safe!
Snakes: We are safe!

Narrator: Noah, his family, and the animals left the ark two by two to start a new life.

Everybody: We are safe! Thank you Noah!

All actors take a bow.

11.
SUNKEN HISTORY: GALLIPOLI SHIPWRECKS

BARRY NICHOLSON

11. SUNKEN HISTORY: GALLIPOLI SHIPWRECKS

Anyone interested in First World War history or diving in the sea will have a fine time around the Gallipoli peninsular, a land mass in western Turkey of approximately thirty kilometres from north to south and twenty-five kilometres from east to west.

During the First World War large numbers of British, French and Italian ships were sunk in the Gallipoli and Canakkale areas of western Turkey. These included war ships, landing craft, and smaller boats called lighters carrying provisions and troops. A large number of Australian and New Zealand soldiers gave their lives in the ensuing land battles, ensuring a steady stream of visitors from these countries to this day.

The Gallipoli campaign started on the 18th of March 1915 when the British navy and its allies sought to attack Istanbul (Constantinople) by the Canakkale Strait. The plan was that troops would land at Gallipoli and capture Turkish positions overlooking the straits. Then, British ships could sail on and capture Constantinople, forcing Turkey to surrender. Their attempt failed, so a joint offensive was launched by British, French and Italian ships on 25th April 1915 in which thousands of troops landed on the peninsula. The landings were concentrated in three places: Anzac Cove and North Beach, Cape Helles, and Sulva Bay. Turkish resistance was unexpectedly strong, partly due to the military skills of Mustafa Kemal Ataturk. This forced an allied withdrawal on the 9th of January 1916.

Some of the blame has to be put on inaccurate maps used by the Allies. The plans of 1915 were based on maps of 1908, in turn based on maps from 1854. For example, the maps showed the area between Plugge's Plateau and Russel's Top to be a flat area, but in reality the two were joined by a mountain ridge which meant a lengthy detour. One hill named 'Hill 971' was supposedly 971 feet high, but in fact was 1,000 feet. As a final example, the compass bearing of the map used by a warship was two degrees out, meaning that shells didn't hit their targets. Despite their faults, the maps continued to be used due to the lack of accurate replacements. Overall the campaign was a disaster for the Allies. Over 44,000 British Empire soldiers were killed, including 8,700 Australians and 2,700 New Zealanders. The death toll for the Turks was 86,000.

Anzac Day, April 25th, is now a major ceremony and media focus. Visitors come in their thousands for the many services at the memorials. 2015 was the 100th Centenary: HM The Queen attended the ceremony at the Cenotaph on Whitehall, London, and The Prince of Wales and Prince Harry attended the service in Gallipoli.

Divers love the area because of the large number and range of wrecks hereabouts. The locations of 216 of these wrecks have been identified. New wrecks are being found all the time, as an article in *The Western Australian* testifies. A Sydney-based archaeological team located several new wrecks off Anzac Cove using sonar technology. They were able to locate the British destroyer HMS Louis in Sulva Bay, and also a barge used to transport dead and wounded soldiers from the beach.

One of the most important wrecks is the 'Lundi', a cargo ship carrying supplies and ammunition, sunk by torpedo fire on 15th April 1915. It is located in Sulva Bay at a depth of twenty seven metres and as such is very accessible to divers. Being largely intact, it is especially noted for its variety of marine life such as lobsters, conger eels, bream, goby and carp fish, aswell as pink and yellow sponges.

Divers are also attracted to the many 'lighters' of the area – small British ships of about twenty metres length that were used to carry provisions and landing troops. As they had an open design they were an easy target and many were sunk by gunfire. There are several at below thirty metres depth for example off Anzac and Morto Coves.

To visit the area, Canakkale is your base. It is a lively and bustling city with a youthful population (university students) and is well-located for visiting both the Gallipoli Peninsular and Troy. Express buses leave Istanbul's main bus terminal several times a day and the journey takes about five hours. There are plenty of places to stay in Canakkale, but book ahead during peak seasons (summer and the annual Anzac celebrations in late April).

There are well-organised tours of the Gallipoli Peninsular that can be booked at your hotel or one of the many tour operators in Canakkale. These tours will typically take you around all the main battle sites and monuments on the peninsula, and day tours will include lunch. Adults who are interested in diving can contact the same tour operators to be put in touch with professional divers who can guide you underwater. Diving in Gallipoli can be colder than other diving destinations in Turkey, but to make up for this, visibility is excellent. The boat ride will take from twenty minutes to an hour to reach the diving sites, and the vast choice of sunken wrecks means two or more sites can be viewed in one day. Nauticalarch.org has a nice little article detailing one group of divers' explorations. They locate anchors, the ship HMS Majestic, and the Lundi.

All in all the Gallipoli area has much to offer the visitor both in and out of the water. For those who are able, diving in the area is a unique experience that combines a variety of interesting marine life with sunken history. Those not interested in nautical pursuits can visit the many battlefield sites and monuments and pay tribute to those who courageously lost their lives back in 1915.

Idea for the Classroom: Sink or Float?

To complement the idea of sunken shipwrecks you can try this activity. How can something that is heavier than water float? It is an activity that contrasts two opposites in a very straightforward way and it is a scientific test – one that involves guesswork and one that children will enjoy.

Fill either a bucket or the class sink with water, about two-thirds full. Make this area as visible as possible to the whole class. Collect a number of objects, some that float and some that do not. Place an object into the water to see if it sinks or floats. It is a good idea to have a guess at whether the object will float or not – possibly even a class vote.

With some things it is easy to tell if they will sink or float, others difficult. Some objects might be the following:

- an egg
- a boiled egg
- an orange
- chalk
- cheese
- chocolate
- a toy ship

As the objects go into the water, make a note of the results – this gives the activity a more scientific slant.

	float	sink
an egg		
a boiled egg		
an orange		
chalk		
cheese		
chocolate		
a toy ship		

Idea for the Classroom: Battleships Game

This is a guessing game that involves skill and strategy, played with two players or in two teams. Each team has a grid of, say, ten by ten squares (see the example below); the horizontal lines are marked one to ten, and the vertical lines marked A to J. Each team has five ships of different sizes: the largest ship is five grid squares long, the next ship four grid squares long, the next three squares long, the next two squares long, and the final just one square long.

To play, each team puts their five ships at random onto their grid making sure the other team does not see where the ships are. You'll have to put a screen of some kind between the two teams (students schoolbags, maybe). Teams take it in turns to call out a grid square, for example "A-5" and if the opponents team has a ship or part of a ship on that square they must call out "hit". Then it is the other team's turn, and so on. If a team manages to guess all the squares the opponent's ship is on then that ship is 'sunk'. The winner is the team to successfully sink all of the opponent's ships.

Idea for the Classroom: Gallipoli Map Annotation

Look at the map and answer the questions.

1. Locate Anzac Cove, North Beach, Cape Helles, Sulva Bay, and the salt lake.
2. Mark on the following wrecks: Lundi (Sulva Bay), HMS Majestic (Anzac Cove), lighters (around Anzac Cove).
3. Locate Hill 971, Battleship Hill, Plugge's Plateau, Chocolate Hill, and Achi Baba Hill.
4. What is the highest peak in the area?
5. Locate the following monuments: Lone Pine Cemetery (just NE of Kabatepe), Anzac Bay Monument (Anzac Cove), the Big Monument (Cape Helles).
6. Allied troops landed at Anzac Cove, North Beach, Cape Helles, and Sulva Bay. With arrows, mark on the landings.
7. Minefields were placed in the narrow strait to the west of Canakkale. Mark the area.
8. Constantinople (modern Istanbul) is in a NE direction through the narrow strait. Put an arrow on the map to show its direction.
9. The map is N-centred. Draw an icon to show N S E and W.
10. Find out what the weather is like in Gallipoli and Canakkale in the four seasons. How is the weather on April 25th?

Map of Gallipoli Peninsula

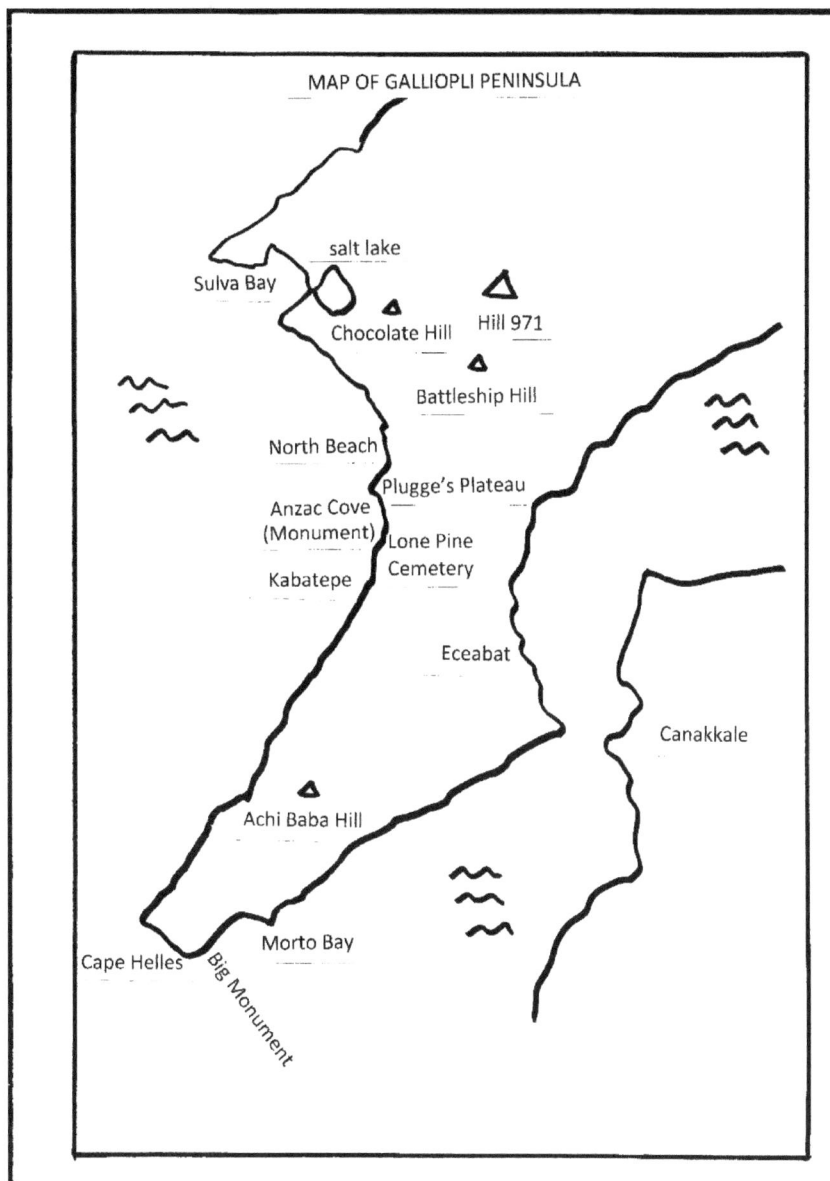

MAP OF GALLIOPLI PENINSULA

salt lake

Sulva Bay

Chocolate Hill

Hill 971

Battleship Hill

North Beach

Plugge's Plateau

Anzac Cove
(Monument)

Lone Pine
Cemetery

Kabatepe

Eceabat

Canakkale

Achi Baba Hill

Morto Bay

Cape Helles

Big Monument

Battleships
Player A

	A	B	C	D	E	F	G	H	I	J
1										
2										
3										
4										
5										
6										
7										
8										
9										
10										

ships:

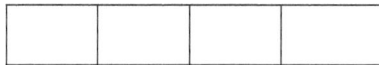

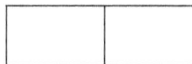

Battleships
Player B

	A	B	C	D	E	F	G	H	I	J
1										
2										
3										
4										
5										
6										
7										
8										
9										
10										

ships:

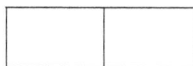

BARRY NICHOLSON

12.
BODRUM MUSEUM
OF
UNDERWATER
ARCHAEOLOGY

12. BODRUM MUSEUM OF UNDERWATER ARCHAEOLOGY

Bodrum is a magical place where the pine-clad mountains with their sugar cube villas meet the sparkling Aegean Sea.

Set in the middle of this is St. Peter's Castle, home to the Museum of Underwater Archaeology, perhaps Bodrum's best tourist attraction and one of the most important underwater archaeology museums in the world. The museum opened in 1964 after several years spent restoring the castle. It is divided into fourteen exhibitions, from the English Tower to the Glass Wreck Hall, and it is overseen by the Institute of Nautical Archaeology (INA), a US non-profit organisation.

I have visited several times and the exhibitions never fail to impress. In particular the two most famous wrecks exhibited at the museum draw my attention: the Uluburun Wreck, and the Glass Wreck.

The Uluburun Hall opened in 1999 and tells the story of this cargo ship and shows off much of its precious cargo. This late Bronze Age ship is the world's oldest known wreck and was discovered by a local sponge diver at Uluburun (near Kas on Turkey's southern coast) in 1982. "Uluburun" is Turkish for "Grand Cape" and reflects how the ship met its fate – in a collision with the headland in strong winds.

Excavations followed: in 1984 under the direction of Prof. Dr. George Bass, and from 1985 to 1995 under the direction of Dr. Cemal Pulak. The wreck was located at a depth of forty-five metres to the stern and fifty-two metres to the bow, making it a very deep wreck and difficult to excavate. Its position on a steep, rocky slope did not help.

The vessel comprises a wooden, single-mast sailing ship, apparently constructed by building the shell first and then fitting the frame to it. Its length is around sixteen metres with twenty-four stone anchors. It is probable that the ship set sail from either a Cypriot or Syrian port with a first destination somewhere on the Aegean Sea (maybe Rhodes) and a final destination in mainland Greece. There was evidently a lot of sea trade in this part of the Mediterranean at that time.

Of most interest to archaeologists is the ship's cargo, a showcase of artefacts from many geographical locations including continental Europe and Africa. On board were found copper, tin and glass ingots, Egyptian jewellery, precious gems, ivory, scrap gold and silver, ostrich eggshells, and a trumpet. Scientists were particularly excited about a solid gold scarab inscribed with the name of Nefertiti which, aswell as being a fine object in itself, helped date the vessel to about 1,300 BC. It sank in about the fourteenth century BC.

The other important display in Bodrum is the Glass Wreck Hall, opened in 1986. Back in 1973 a local sponge diver guided members of the INA to Serce Limani, a remote headland jutting out into the Aegean Sea, twenty-four miles west of Marmaris. The wreck was found at a depth of thirty-two metres.

It was excavated between 1977-1979 by Prof. Dr. Bass and his team of twenty US and Turkish divers and scientists. Excavation was a slow task as the glass was often stuck together with silt and sand, and the water was very murky. In addition it was only possible to dive in pairs and for a maximum of twenty minutes because of the poor conditions. They even had to contend with a giant unfriendly octopus that came to inspect the divers work!

The vessel was sixteen metres long and propelled by two large sails, and was built by nailing planks onto a skeletal frame (in contrast to the Uluburun wreck). Its flat bottom made it particularly suitable for river navigation, and it had a capacity of thirty-five tons. It had probably set sail from Syria and was making its way to a glass smelting factory within the Byzantine Empire.

In fact that was its main cargo – glass. It held broken glass and glass ingots stored in sacks and baskets, and to this day remains the largest collection of Islamic glass ever found. Archaeologists estimate that there were around ten thousand glass objects on board, of which only eighty were found intact. Scientists sorted the shards into over a dozen categories according to colour and decoration. They were able to reconstruct glass bowls, bottles, pitchers, plates, and jars, and from these dated the wreck to about 1025 AD.

Bodrum is easy to get to by air, bus, or by sea. Bodrum-Milas Airport serves both domestic flights to Istanbul and Ankara and international flights to the UK and Germany amongst others. There are more flights in the summer as the area is a popular package holiday destination. Express buses run regularly from Izmir and Antalya, less frequently from Istanbul and Ankara. The most enjoyable and exciting way to arrive is by sea. If your pockets are as deep as the Aegean then moor your boat in Bodrum Harbour for an appropriate fee. The rest of us can enjoy the regular ferry service from the Greek island of Kos. It takes under an hour and is not expensive. Using Bodrum town as your base, there are plenty of accommodation options to suit all budgets.

You can not miss St. Peter's Castle on a picturesque headland right in the centre of town. For a modest fee visitors can tour the castle, but unfortunately entrance to some of the exhibition halls requires an extra fee. For me, the location is enough!

Idea for the Classroom: Pirate Hats

One of the easiest ways to disguise yourself in fancy dress is to make a pirate's hat. You'll need a piece of A4 coloured paper to start. Draw a wavy line down the middle of the paper as shown in the diagram below. Cut down the line, and stick or staple the two halves together to make a hat shape. Draw a skull and crossbones onto the front of the hat to complete the effect. A sword and shield can be made from paper or card and, ah, Jim lad, your children are transformed into pirates. Pieces of eight!

Idea for the Classroom: Message in a Bottle

Did you hear the story of Robinson Crusoe? He was stranded for many years on a tropical island in the middle of nowhere and was only saved when someone found his message in a bottle asking for help.

There are two ways to do this activity in the classroom. First, as a role-play pretending to be stranded on a tropical island. Imagine you are Robinson Crusoe. What would you write in your letter? Probably you would say something about how you got onto the island (plane crash, ship wreck), a description of the island (mountains, rocks, sand, beaches, vegetation), how you are managing to survive (food, shelter) and a plea to be rescued. Try writing something like the following example:

MESSAGE IN A BOTTLE

Please help!

My name is Robinson Crusoe and I am stranded on a tropical island.

I was travelling on the ship Mayflower 2 when suddenly there was a big storm and the ship sank. When I woke up I was on a sandy beach on this deserted island. There were no other survivors.

There is nothing much on the island, only a mountain and palm trees. There is one sandy beach. I found a stream and a small waterfall where I can wash. I walked around the island this morning and it took about an hour. It is a very boring place!

I live in a cave. I share the cave with some small friendly animals – I think they are rats. Mostly I eat fish from the sea, berries, nuts, and green plants. I know how to make fire and can cook the food well, but I really miss chocolate and ice-cream.

Please, please, please... if you find this message then come and rescue me! I want to go home. I want to see my family.

Yours,

Robinson Crusoe.

Secondly, you could search for new friends around the world by writing an introduction to yourself and put your school name and class so that the finder can contact you. This is a much more interesting method, but it may take years before you get a reply, if at all! Try the following example:

MESSAGE IN A BOTTLE

Hello, my name is _____ and this is my message in a bottle.

I am _____ years old and live in _____. My favourite football team is _____ and my favourite food is _____. I have _____ brothers and _____ sister. My best friend is _____.

Please, if you find my message in a bottle please reply to Class ___, _____ Primary School, London, England.

What is your name? Where do you live? How old are you?

Your new friend,

Barry.

Idea for the Classroom: Treasure Chest

You are going to make a time capsule and bury it in the school garden for a future generation to dig up and examine, and we're going to call it a Treasure Chest.

First find a strong and sturdy steel box that all the objects can go into, and then start making a list of possible things to go into the box. You might want to include things from your school such as a text book or pencil case with a picture of a famous pop star on it, or you might include something from daily life like a newspaper or item of clothing. It is a good idea to put some children's artwork in the box too. Some things are not suitable for a time capsule – food and drink, anything that will decompose, or anything too big to fit into the box.

Once the treasure chest is prepared and sealed, it is time to dig a hole and bury it in the school garden. It doesn't need to be too deep – a foot is enough – but is does need to be away from risk of flood or tunnelling animals. Set a date on which the capsule is to be dug up, say, twenty years into the future. Importantly, draw a treasure map so that a future generation can locate the chest. Finally, do some research on whether there were any similar time capsules buried twenty years ago, as maybe you will be able to locate them and dig them up – real treasure!

Pirate Hat

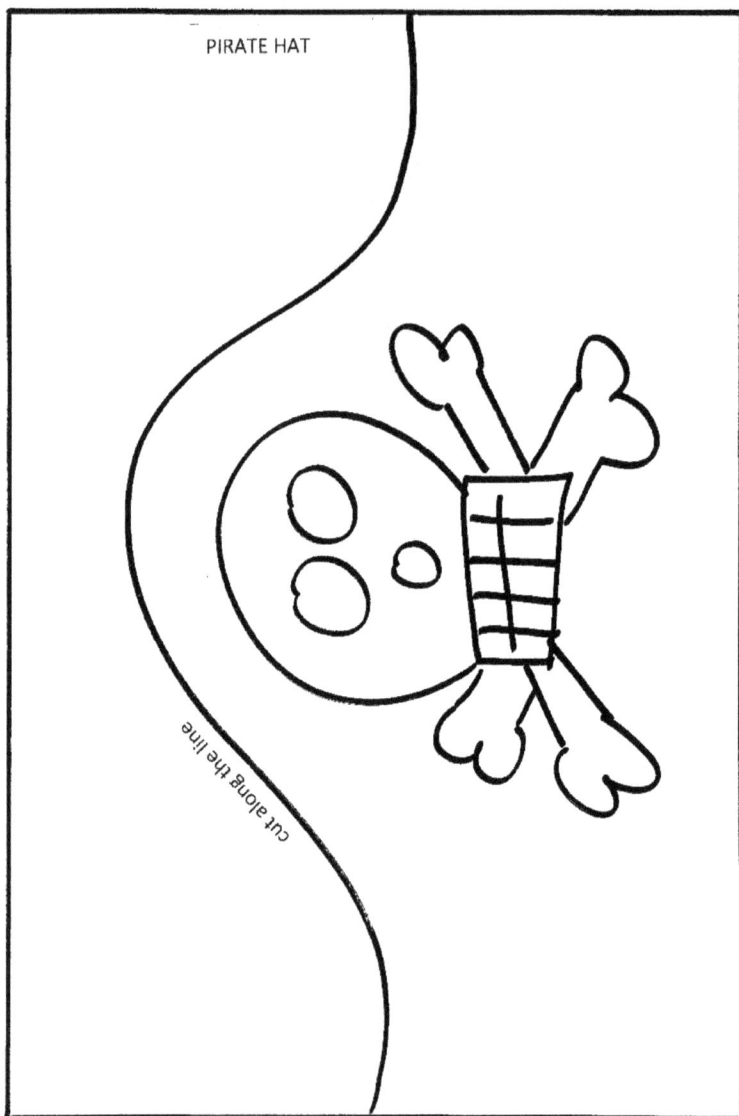

CONCLUSION

Turkey is a beautiful country with a long history. Why not bring some of this rich cultural heritage into the classroom? I've made a start for you with what I feel to be a good range of interesting stories and some relevant activities that bring the tales to real life.

Most of the tales presented here have some geographical basis. If you can, go to these places, visit these places, and preferably with children. Failing that, there is a huge amount of information on the internet. Many websites have excellent pictures, so you can go to these places 'virtually'.

Take heed of the morals and lessons some of the stories have. Don't be greedy like King Midas; take warnings from God or fortune tellers seriously; try not to let cultural assets such as ancient cities be forgotten or destroyed.

Above all, try some of the activities and crafts and let your students enjoy them in a creative way, and experience some of the true drama and excitement of these tales from Turkey. Please enjoy the stories and activities in this book with all your heart: your children will love you for it.

Barry Nicholson
Istanbul 2015

BARRY NICHOLSON

REFERENCES

The Wooden Horse of Troy

global.britannica.com (story and background)
greece.mrdon.org (story)
historyforkids.org (background and the Trojan Horse story)
web.stanford.edu (historical background)
wikipedia.com (background)

King Midas and his Golden Touch

childstoryhour.com (tells the story in a child-like way)
greeka.com (the wish, the curse, the atonement)
livius.org (proverbial meaning)
mythweb.com (proverbial meaning)
primaryresources.co.uk (comical cartoon story)
shmoop.com (divides into a 'short story' and a 'long story')
wikipedia.com (background, and outline of myth)

Saint Nicholas and the Three Pickled Boys

britishfoodabout.com (pickled onions recipe)
canterbury-cathedral.org (St. Nicholas Day Parade)
catholic.org (background and life)
food.com (pickled onions recipe)
itv.com (photos of Canterbury's St. Nicholas Day)
newadvent.org (background and life)
stnicholascentre.org (pickled boys story, modern tourism)
wikipedia.com (pickled boys story, background and life)

The Grey Wolf Legend

animalfactguide.com (facts and information)
europeisnotdead.com (background and legend)
ilovewerewolves.com (brief information)
naturemappingfoundation.org (information and facts)
nps.gov (Yellowstone National Park wolves)
wikipedia.com (Turkish mythology and folklore)
wolf.org (fun wolf facts)
worldwildlife.org (facts and information)
yellowstonenationalpark.com (wolf information)

Turkish Dragons

Aslan, Ferhat 'Dragon Motif in Anatolian Legends' (good background, Sky Dragon legend)
Cambridge Dictionary (online definition)
dragondreaming.wordpress.com (the Persian Dragon)
travelchinaguide.com (Zodiac information)
whats-your-sign.com (Zodiac and personality)
wikipedia.com (brief mention of Turkish dragons)

Maiden's Castle, Istanbul

allaboutturkey.com (background)
ibb.gov.tr (background and history)
maidenscastleandtower.wordpress.com (legend and background)
tkcomenius.webs.com (story)
tripadvisor.com (information about the restaurant)

Akdamar Island, Van

allaboutturkey.com (history, description of church)
armeniapedia.org (Tamar legend)
ecm11van.org (background, Tamar legend)
Hurriyet Daily News April 11-12 2015 'More Armenian Churches Go Under Restoration' (background)
intheknowtraveller.com (Tamar legend, how to get there)
petersommer.com (background, reliefs, how to get there)
roughguides.com (reliefs, what to do)
sacred-destinations.com (history and restoration, what to see)
sacredsites.com (Tamar legend, reliefs)
wikipedia.com (background, restoration)

The Deserted Ghost City of Ani

Hurriyet Daily News April 11-12 2015 'More Armenian Churches Go Under Restoration' (background)
kuriositas.com (brief information)
theatlantic.com (background and history)
virtualani.org (map, history, description and photos)
wikitravel.org (history, visitor information)

Mount Nemrut's Statues of the Past

alaturkaturkey.com (history and description)
atasteoftravelblog.com (background, getting there)
tripadvisor.com (visitor reviews)
unesco.org (history, description, management of site)
wikipedia.com (background, history, facts and figures)

Noah's Ark, Mount Arafat

dailymail.co.uk 28th April 2010 'We've found Noah's Ark!'
sunnyskyz.com 13th December 2013 'Noah's Ark Has Been Found'
The Telegraph 3rd April 2014 'Noah's Ark Would Have Floated'
tkcomenius.webs.com (story, recipe)
viewzone.com/noahx.html (photos, diagrams)

Gallipoli Shipwrecks

allaboutturkey.com (diving-related description)
awm.gov.au (inaccurate maps)
britishlegion.org.uk (Anzac Day ceremonies)
discover.com (Lundi wreck)
diveadvisor.com (diving information)
dl.nfsa.gov.au (history)
gallipoli.gov.au (history, maps, visiting today)
Lonely Planet Turkey (accommodation information)
nauticalarch.org (one diving group's explorations)
The Western Australian, 20th June 2010, 'Divers Discover Gallipoli Wrecks'

Turkish Pirates, Bodrum
bodrum-museum.com (Glass Wreck)
bodrumturkeytravel.com (background, Ulumburu Wreck, Glass Wreck)
kultur.gov.tr (Ulumburu Wreck, Glass Wreck)
saudiaramcoworld.com (Glass Wreck in detail)
thebestofbodrum.com (background to Bodrum, how to get there)
wikipedia.com (Ulumburu Wreck in detail)

BARRY NICHOLSON

ABOUT THE AUTHOR

Born and educated in the United Kingdom, Barry Nicholson holds a Master's degree in Teaching English as a Foreign Language from the University of Reading. During his career abroad, he has taught in the Far east, Germany, Turkey and Poland. His first book 'Practical English Summercamp Activities' was published in June 2015. He currently lives in Istanbul, Turkey.

From the same author

Practical English Summercamp Activities

Starhands Publishing June 2015

ISBN: 9780993243806

If you want to ensure your students are not just parroting the right answers but actually absorbing the lessons you're teaching them, then allow educator Barry Nicholson to reveal his proven educational method:

ACTIVE FUN + LEARNING = SUCCESS

Whether you're teaching English as a foreign language or working with students who have special needs, this book provides you with more than one hundred enjoyable ways to engage your students in the classroom. Better yet, each activity leaves room for your own creative adjustments and can be adapted to fit your lessons.

Student participation is essential in any educational environment, and with this invaluable resource, you can make learning fun and easy for you and your students!

BARRY NICHOLSON